THE TERROR WI

Belfast. A city torn by strife and violence.

But not dangerous enough for Billy McIlwaine.

He also set about destroying himself with alcohol.

Then, in hospital at the point of death, something happened—something that changed his life permanently.

With the help of daughter Rhonda, Billy tells his plain, unvarnished story.

The Terror Within

Billy McIlwaine
with Rhonda McIlwaine

A LION PAPERBACK

Oxford · Batavia · Sydney

Copyright © Billy McIlwaine 1991

Published by
Lion Publishing plc
Peter's Way, Sandy Lane West, Oxford, England
ISBN 0 7459 1875 1
Albatross Books
PO Box 320, Sutherland, NSW 2232, Australia
ISBN 0 7324 0299 9

First edition 1991

British Library Cataloguing in Publication Data
McIlwaine, Billy
The terror within
1. Alcoholism – Biographies
I. Title II. McIlwaine, Rhonda
362.292092
ISBN 0-7459-1875-1

Printed and bound in Great Britain by Cox & Wyman Ltd,
Reading

Contents

Author's Preface

This book was written while I was studying in the United States, based on extensive conversations with my dad before I left. The writing would not have been possible without the support and prayers of my friends there.

I would like to thank my room-mate and friend, Kim Powell, for putting up with me and for patiently listening to many readings of the manuscript. Thanks also to Richard Pitt and David Willis for the use of their computers, and especially to my friend Craig Hargenrader for help with the typing and constant encouragement.

I pay tribute to my mum and dad for showing such confidence in my abilities as to ask me to write this book, and for trusting me with the details of their lives.

Most of all I thank God, with whom 'all things are possible'.

Rhonda McIlwaine

Foreword

This story is so moving because it is for real. It has been my privilege to know Billy McIlwaine through much of the time the story covers, so I can vouch for its reality.

The focal point of the story is the extraordinary encounter Billy experienced in the Mater Hospital. That experience turned his life around in many ways, but not least in lifting him from the pit of alcoholic dependence.

Starting from the hard drinking of army life, his alcoholism grew bleaker and bleaker as his life home in Belfast went on, until, on the verge of death, his life changed.

But the story does not stop there. We read how his personality has been rebuilt since then, and how he has become the man he is now.

Billy would say he owes it all to God's grace, and I agree with him. But his wife and daughter have played a strong part. Sally went through all the anguish and frustration which only other wives of alcoholics can fully appreciate, and she was still there to help with the rebuilding. And daughter Rhonda, born just at the darkest time and now a lively college girl, has written the story in gripping detail.

I recommend this book to all who may be battling beneath the dark cloud of alcoholism. It will show them that there is hope to be found.

T.J. Hagan
The Manse, Donacloney

1
Prisoner

A hazy, unreal world confronts me. In the dim light, I see white-clad figures floating across the room. They stop and gaze in my direction. Who are they? Why do they keep watching me? Am I some kind of a caged animal in a zoo or a type of experiment that must be under constant surveillance? The blurred figures approach me. I turn away, blinded by their white rays. A cold sweat floods my forehead as the menacing shapes come closer and closer. I must escape from this place and its sinister inhabitants.

I am lying on a flat surface. I try to sit up, but I cannot move. I'm shackled to an assortment of tubes and drips and fenced in by iron bars. While struggling to free myself, I suddenly look up. They have arrived. A thousand pairs of eyes burn through me.

'What are his chances of pulling through?' a voice rings through my head.

'I'm afraid there's no hope.'

The figures are looking at me, they are talking about me. A mad panic erupts inside me. I'm going to die.

2
Early Days

Twenty years of alcohol abuse had brought me to this critical moment in Belfast's Mater Hospital in July 1979. My body was being destroyed by the killer disease cirrhosis of the liver. I had been in hospital before and for a long time I had been aware that death was imminent, but I had visualized going out in a drunken blaze of glory. Now, all I faced was a biting fear of the grave and what lay beyond.

My love affair with the booze began when I was about fifteen years old, and I remember vividly my first encounter with alcohol. Standing in a shadowy alleyway with some other boys, we passed round a bottle of cheap wine as if it were some precious treasure. Each of us took a swig out of the bottle and our screwed-up faces showed our reaction. The booze was horrible, there was no pleasure in the taste—yet drinking it gave us young lads a hard tough image and made us feel grown-up. In the midst of adolescence we needed an identity, and our little drinking session seemed to give us that.

I didn't get drunk on that occasion, but soon afterwards I went to a dance with a guy called Desy who lived in a neighbouring street. Before going to the dance we headed for a pub for a quick drink. But a couple of pints soon turned into a full-scale drinking session and I ended up drunk. It was a horrific experience. My whole world was spinning, nothing was secure or stable any more and I clung desperately to the walls of the buildings as we walked towards the booming dance hall. The menacing-looking bouncers on the door noted the state I was in.

'Clear off! There's no way you're coming in here!'

Desy appeared to know one of them.

'Look mate, he's not out to cause trouble. So maybe he's had one too many, but I'll guarantee his good behaviour, if you'll let us in.'

With this they relented. But such a promise was unnecessary—I wasn't fit to cause trouble and spent most of the night in the toilets being violently sick and vowing never again to touch alcohol.

But the horror of intoxication soon faded from memory; my promise, though sincere at the time, proved to be short-lived. Like cigarettes and drugs, alcohol is a magnet which draws you back to try again. Before long you're hooked, trapped in a vicious circle, from which it is almost impossible to escape.

My teenage years were a whirl of dances and drinking. I was part of a gang which hung around the Crownville Snooker Hall on Belfast's Shankill Road. One of our favourite haunts was the Tudor Hall, a riotous establishment, where flare-ups between rival gangs were part of a night's entertainment. We passed through its doors about three or four times a week decked out in our Teddy boy gear—velvet-collared coats, drainpipe trousers and huge thick-soled shoes! The usual procedure was to ply ourselves with booze before entering the crowded dance hall. Then, our nerves steadied, we asked girls for a quick jive to the strains of Fats Domino and Little Richard. Very often a crowd from Ardoyne, a predominantly Republican area, would be present, and after a few drinks we were ready to tackle them. The brawls between Shankill

Road Protestants and Ardoyne Catholics were part of life and tensions ran high even in those days before the Troubles began.

One particular night I challenged a guy from Ardoyne and without saying a word he grabbed my shirt, ripped it off my back and thumped me on the head. Reeling with pain, I didn't know what had hit me.

'What am I going to do? I can't go home in this state,' I thought.

Frightened at the thought of my mother's fury when she saw my bedraggled appearance, I raced off to a friend's house to get cleaned up and sew my tattered shirt before confronting her.

Drink often spawned the sectarian fighting. One evening I was arrested after a skirmish in the Crumlin Road. The police swooped and I was grabbed, bundled into a van and taken off to the nearest police station, where I was detained. The room was dim; I was lectured by an imposing-looking cop, each word making me squirm in my seat.

'Look, McIlwaine, there is no excuse for this fighting. You've committed a very serious offence and we will more than likely be taking you to court. They'll sort you out there all right!'

However, this threat was never carried out, much to my relief. The police realized that the framing of one individual would not halt the Catholic/Protestant brawls. But that's all they were—kicks and punches, a result of pent-up brutality. No killings: it was just a case of rival gangs fighting each other.

Drinking proved an expensive habit and money was hard to come by in those days. Although at fifteen I was earning money, most of it went towards my keep and I was left with usually about half a crown for 'pocket money'. To boost my resources I used to run errands for neighbours. Another of my money-making schemes

14

was to act as look-out for what was called the 'Pitch and Toss'—illegal gambling sessions which were popular in working-class areas. These were usually held in the street or on a piece of waste ground—a group of men huddled together, eagerly awaiting the outcome of the tossing of two coins. The fear of a police sweep prompted the participants to employ look-outs, so I and some mates stood on the corner and scanned the area for R.U.C. uniforms. The shout of 'Cops' put a premature halt to the gambling and the place was soon cleared of all traces of the illegal act. When the session was finished we were given some money for our services. The money soon disappeared into the cash register of the local off-licence or was used to go to a dance. Because of the sectarian fighting at the dances, there was safety in numbers, so in the gang we helped each other out, lending money to those who were broke.

After leaving school at fourteen, I had had various jobs, ranging from messenger boy in the stationery department of Belfast's City Hall to working in a butcher's shop. That job only lasted for half a day; I made a quick departure after watching sausages being made and vowed never again to eat meat. I also worked in various mills around Belfast and was usually stationed at the gatehouse. I enjoyed this—it was good to be out in the fresh air far from the claustrophobic factory atmosphere.

It was during my time at Edenderry Mill on the Crumlin Road that I had another run-in with the law. As usual, I was trying to acquire money for booze. It was a grey wet day and I was on one of my frequent visits to Belfast city centre delivering letters to other companies. I bustled along the shiny streets clad in a long waterproof cape, probably looking like an oversized garden gnome. The sheets of rain got heavier so I darted into Woolworths in the High

Street. It was warm and dry inside and the relaxing music was a welcome contrast to the weather. I strolled along the lanes taking a leisurely look at the goods displayed on the shelves. After about fifteen minutes I found myself in the DIY section and spotted some pliers like those I had seen the engineers in the mill using. Suddenly, on instinct, I grabbed a few pairs of the pliers and, after checking that no one was watching, stuffed them under my long raincoat. It may have looked ridiculous, but it made an excellent hiding-place. 'This is dead easy,' I thought triumphantly. 'I'll sell these pliers to the engineers and use the money to buy some booze.'

Feeling very pleased with my little scheme, I strolled towards the exit trying not to look suspicious. But, just as I was about to push open the swing door, I felt a heavy hand on my shoulder and heard an unfriendly voice in my ear.

'Would you please accompany me to the manager's office. I have reason to believe that you have been shoplifting.'

My scheme had failed. The store detective had seen everything. I was marched off to the manager's office where I was searched; the pliers were soon found to be in my possession and the police were called in. After being charged I went home to face my distraught mother.

'You're a disgrace, Billy. You've ruined the good reputation of this family! No one has ever been in trouble before this!'

I was taken to court but was put on probation for two years, much to the relief of my anxious mother. From that time on, when I was going out to dances she warned me not to get into trouble, knowing I could end up in gaol.

Looking back, I can see that my teenage drinking probably had its roots in my father's actions and my home environment. I was born on 10 March 1943, one of eleven children, and grew up on the Shankill Road, a hardline Loyalist district of Belfast. My father, also called William, was a thin wiry man and a chronic alcoholic. I remember him sending those of us who were old enough to Ward's, a local wine store which was situated on the edge of the Republican Falls Road. The thought of venturing into this dangerous area terrified us and often we tried to talk our way out of it: 'Oh please Daddy, send somebody else, one of the older ones. I might get caught by the Catholics. They'll beat me up!'

Most of the time our pleas were in vain and we obliged rather than defy my father.

When it was my turn to go, I saw the whole event as a race. I sprinted along Couper Street towards the Falls, as if being chased by some invisible pursuer. After quickly handing over 4/6 for a bottle of cheap wine, I dashed the whole way back, carrying the bottle wrapped in brown paper under one arm, only slowing down when I reached the safety of my own area.

This visit to the off-licence was a daily excursion. My father needed drink constantly and liked to drink at home rather than standing in pubs. So in many ways I can see in him the roots of my own alcohol problem. My earliest memories of my dad always connected him with alcohol. Like all children, I was vulnerable and highly impressionable, ready to imitate the 'big people' in my life, such as parents and leaders. People in such positions have a responsibility to set a high standard; if they indulge in drinking or other vices this gives a licence to young people to do so. I sometimes wonder if anyone copied my life-style... a frightening thought.

Our household was a poor one, money always in short supply, yet my father always found enough for drink. Thirteen of us were squashed into a tiny matchbox of a house. With only two bedrooms, my parents slept in one and the children in the other, squeezed into two double beds. Very often I woke up in the morning with someone's toe in my mouth! Home comforts and luxuries were few, we lived on the bare essentials. A shower or bath was unknown; for something like that one had to visit the local swimming baths. Most of the time we used a large stone sink filled with water from a kettle for washing. This we called the 'jaw box' and during the hectic weekends of our youth we had to queue up to use it. Food was cheap and basic. Sunday was the best day of the week as the smell of sizzling bacon wafted from the kitchen. On Thursdays my sister Clara brought home a veritable feast of broken biscuits from the factory where she worked. But these were our only luxuries. Life was a struggle, but through the deceptive haze of alcohol it seemed possible to escape from the poverty, an illusion which I and my father both possessed.

Before my drinking career began I was involved in a local pentecostal church. After experiencing a Christian conversion at eleven, I and several other boys—Alastair McComish, Eddie Playfair and Sammy Grant—held frequent open air meetings on the Shankill Road and many people became Christians. Full of zeal we attended as many meetings as we could each week. We were also part of a scout troop and generally our whole lives revolved around church.

Looking back, I can see that God did a great deal for me during my early teenage years. One Saturday afternoon I was walking to a football match when suddenly a car mounted the pavement, pushing me to the ground. This left me temporarily paralyzed and affected my nervous system. Often I experienced a sharp loss of breath and thought I was dying. My mother, frantic with worry, took me to numerous doctors, but to no avail. However, when I started going to church it seemed to settle my nerves and relax my body.

Another thing which caused my mother great anxiety was my perforated ear-drum. It bled nightly and each morning I awoke to find a blood-soaked pillow. In the late fifties a great healing rally was held in the Wellington Hall in central Belfast. I joined the healing line and was soon confronted with the American evangelist who was conducting the rally.

'Do you believe God can heal you, son?' he asked in a slow southern drawl.

I answered in the affirmative and immediately his hands were upon me and I felt an intense heat scorching through my body. I knew instinctively that I had been healed even though there was no visible sign of healing. The following evening I related this to a sceptical doctor. After shining a light into my ear, he was forced to agree with me. God had succeeded where the medical profession had failed. My ear-drum was perfect.

God had made a huge impact on my early teenage life and my drinking proved to be a total turn-around. I had become disillusioned with the Christian life and I had made the fundamental mistake of failing to keep my sights fixed on Jesus, and beginning to look with critical eyes at other people. Many of the individuals I knew were half-hearted, not totally committed to the church, and this led me to believe that perhaps the Christian life was empty and futile. My whole spiritual life deteriorated and I stopped reading the Bible, praying and attending meetings. This was the start of what later became a road to self-destruction.

First, my teenage drinking led to a sharp deterioration in my relationship with my father, which later I was to regret deeply. One night I arrived home very late from a dance, after an evening of drinking and brawling. My father was waiting up for me.

'Where have you been to this hour?' he bellowed.

'None of your business, I can do what I like!' I snarled.

But before I knew what had hit me my father had removed his belt and was thrashing me with it. Each piercing lash increased my resentment towards him—I never spoke to him again.

A few weeks later I arrived home from work, weary after a hard day's toil in the moulding shop of Mackie's Foundry. I was greeted by my mother's tear-stained face; Mr Armstrong, a neighbour, was trying to comfort her.

'What's wrong?' I inquired anxiously, knowing that my mother was not easily reduced to tears.

'It's your father, Billy; he's in bed very ill. Your mum's a bit upset.'

These sombre words sent shivers down my spine as I realized I wasn't speaking to my dad. What if something happened to him? He would die thinking I didn't love him. Haunted by such thoughts I rushed upstairs. But it was too late. A white sheet covered the bed—underneath was the outline of my father's frail body.

'But he can't be dead. It's not true!' I inwardly screamed.

I heard a shuffling behind me and felt a hand on my shoulder; it was Mr Armstrong.

'I'm so sorry, son, but at least he's in no more pain. I haven't told your mother yet; I'll wait until some of the others get home.'

These words swam around me; I was locked in my own little world, numbed by the shock that I had never made up with my father—we were eternally separated.

Full of remorse, I swore that never again would I stop speaking to someone. But I was unable to shake off the feelings of guilt. I found our home unbearable to live in, each room filled with memories of my father. My mother's wretched face, etched with lines, was a constant reminder of our loss. I had to get away from Belfast—the army seemed to be the answer.

3

Army Life

My brother Charlie had painted a glorious and exciting picture of the Territorial Army, so I decided to follow in his footsteps and join. As I forged my age on the crisp white forms I thought of the good times that lay ahead. Annual camps in England and Wales, good pay, lots of girls and an abundance of booze. I was only sixteen.

After I had passed the medical the TA accepted me into their ranks as part of the A-company of the Royal Ulster Rifles based at Whitehouse, a few miles outside Belfast. For two years I went to the Territorials twice weekly. In addition, we set off every weekend for places such as Magilligan. It was great to get out of the smoky city into the open fields and breathe in the fresh clean air. Rifle practice, boxing and other sporting pursuits took up most of our time but we still found opportunities to drink. Almost every weekend camp turned into a boozing session and I began to plunge deeper and deeper into that way of life.

One particular autumn weekend my company was camping at Magilligan in the northern part of Northern Ireland. Some friends and I decided to go for a trip into Portrush, a nearby seaside resort on the beautiful Antrim coast. However, the only part of the town that we saw was the inside of its bars, as we embarked on our usual pub crawl. Totally stoned, I made a remark to one of the men I was with and suddenly found myself plunged into blackness. Waking up on the ground outside Barry's Amusements, I realized that I must have made a pretty provocative remark to deserve such a punch! I ached physically and mentally, knowing I had insulted somebody and suffered the consequences. Since then, I've seen many people saying things they don't mean because alcohol has robbed them of their full mental faculties. Like me, people lose control of their minds and mouths when drunk.

The advent of summer signified camps outside Northern Ireland, and one of them was spent at Tenby on the Pembrokeshire coast. A typical night was usually a drinking spree in the small Welsh town, after which I and my pals returned to camp famished and raided the cookhouse for any scraps of food we could lay our hands on. Cards were another important part of TA life and many nights were filled with tense poker and pontoon games.

All this was a far cry from my humble upbringing in 98 Wilton Street: the TA showed me there was a wild side of life and I wanted it. So one afternoon, two years after joining the Territorials, I managed to summon up the courage and pushed open the door of Clifton Street recruiting office in the centre of Belfast.

'I... ahh... want to join the army, sir,' I stuttered nervously to the officer sitting behind the desk.

Half an hour later I emerged from the office clutching a batch of official-looking papers. My dream was to join the driving division, and the recruiting officer had advised me to apply for the Royal Army Service Corps. At that time I was totally infatuated with cars. No one in my family had ever possessed one and I was dying to get behind a wheel. I thought perhaps if I could learn to drive in the army, at some stage I could buy my own car.

After a test and medical, I was forced to wait

patiently for the results. That week seemed to stretch endlessly. Finally, Friday morning arrived and so did a formal looking brown envelope. Nervously I tore it open. I ran into the scullery where my mother stood leaning over the 'jaw box'.

'Ma, I'm gonna be a soldier!' I screamed with delight.

But the initial excitement soon faded and the day of my departure brought great sadness. Standing with my mother, brothers and sisters on the dockside, I realized that family ties were to be severed; I was going out into the big wide world on my own. Soon my ship was pulling out of Belfast Lough and I knew I was leaving my whole world behind me. Straight away I headed for the bar and ordered a drink, hoping this would be some kind of consolation for the loneliness which was sweeping over me already. I spent most of the journey staring at the bottom of a beer glass. Several hours and many drinks later the ship docked at Heysham. I stepped off straight on to a train heading for Buller Barracks at Aldershot, where I was to spend the next six weeks in training.

The stark grey facade of the training depot reminded me of a Second World War prison camp; what was I letting myself in for? As I neared the camp, shouts and screams pierced the air, sending shivers down my spine. I listened to the sergeant major's booming voice as he humiliated man after man in public. It was then that I knew I had made a mistake. I walked across the parade ground and his attention was suddenly on me.

'Stop looking round, you silly fool! Hold your head up and march over to reception!'

After collecting my bedding I was introduced to the NCO and the other new recruits, several of whom were also from Northern Ireland. As I looked at the frightened, pale faces, I realized that everyone felt the same way; the army certainly was not what we expected.

A few days later I looked at myself in a mirror, clad in khaki, my hair shorn. Was it really me? A total identity change had taken place. The army was a shock all right, especially in terms of physical endurance. Day and night our feet pounded the grey tarmac of the parade ground until we were ready to drop.

Cross-country running was another feature of military training. At last, here was something which I enjoyed doing. I loved that surge of power, that exhilaration that came from sprinting. I got the chance to show off my speed at a sports open day in the camp. One of the events was a three-mile race. My humble rubber-soled shoes, army shorts and vest contrasted strongly with the expensive running gear of the other competitors. But I was determined to beat them.

We crouched down on the starting line, our minds geared towards that elusive trophy. Then suddenly the gun cracked; we were off! I bolted while the other runners paced themselves. Within seconds I was surging far in front of the others towards the first line.

'Come on, McIlwaine! Come on!' my platoon shouted.

I decided to ease off and let the runners think that they had a chance, then I spurted off again, dashing their hopes of success. Their trendy sports gear did little for their speed, as I won the race hands down. As I crossed the finishing line a roar of delight erupted from my platoon; no Olympic athlete could have got a better reception.

My platoon commanders felt I had real potential and encouraged me to continue training for other events. So running played a big part in my life in the army. It taught me discipline and stamina and was a positive input in my life. In stark contrast, my boozing habits continued and were heightened by the military regime. The NAAFI became my second home. Fights flared up almost every night. I was involved in a few but really tried to keep my nose clean as the army hierarchy took a dim view of brawling.

For six long weeks I endured Aldershot's gruelling regime. Regular square-bashing, learning how to use a 303 rifle, Bren gun and other firearms were the rudiments of military life. I quickly learned how to be a soldier, how to engage in combat if necessary. Basic training was soon over and passing-out day dawned. Many of the other recruits' families came to see them. But there was no one to watch me pass out, no one to take pride in my achievement; my family couldn't afford to make the journey to England.

Although it had been my ambition to join the army and learn how to drive, it really wasn't all I thought it would be. Depressed and homesick, I scrawled a begging letter to my mother asking her to pay the twenty pounds which would release me from my misery. But money was in short supply in my family and I decided I would have to make the best of a bad job.

My next base was a driver training camp in Yeovil, Somerset. In many ways this was a more relaxed kind of camp, the regulations were not as strict. I found myself trying to drive Austin K4 trucks, which was a real challenge. The crash gear boxes of these three-ton trucks made them extremely difficult to handle. The same could also be said for my driving instructor. A bit of a disagreement blew up between us over my progress. I thought I'd done sufficiently well to attempt a driving test, but he thought differently. Eventually he relented. I took the test and failed. This happened a second time and I was advised to transfer to the Amphibs division.

'I don't think that you're meant for this division,' my commanding officer told me. 'Perhaps you should transfer to where you would be better suited.'

'Look sir, give me one more chance,' I pleaded. 'I'll try harder. Just let me have another try at the driving test and if I fail this time I'll go into Amphibs.'

He agreed and I took the test again. Much to my relief I sailed through it this time. I was now an army driver.

Much of my time in Somerset was spent boozing, drinking the local scrumpy. I remember vividly my outing to see Acker Bilk, a popular jazz musician of the time. Beforehand I plied myself with booze at a local pub. Several pints of scrumpy later I decided to go to the concert. But once outside the pub, my knees buckled under me and the next thing I knew I was lying on the ground surrounded by blue-uniformed policemen. Eventually I managed to get to the concert hall, but my night was spent not jiving on the dance floor but slumped in a corner, head pounding and feeling very sick. I vowed never again to touch scrumpy, but as usual this promise didn't last very long. My memory quickly faded and I returned to my old drinking habits.

After several weeks of intensive training the time came for us to be posted to our permanent units. I knew I could be sent almost anywhere in the world. We were given some leave and I returned home to my family and girlfriend. It was great to be back and I spent the next couple of weeks partying and having a good time. The time whizzed by fast, and I was reluctant to return to the discipline of army life. I dreamed up some imaginary back pains and paid a visit to the doctor, who was totally taken in by my little scheme. My leave was extended by a couple of weeks and then I was saying goodbye to my family and friends.

Back in Yeovil I found myself pretty much alone, as most of my friends had been given their postings and had flown off to far-flung countries such as Singapore, Aden and Germany. Because of my late return most of the postings were gone; only one was left—Kenya!

I was given a little more leave. The word spread like wildfire at home: 'Billy McIlwaine is going to the wilds of Africa!' Everyone thought it was very exciting that a boy from the back streets of Belfast should be travelling so far, but I thought differently. Within a short time I was in a transit camp in England preparing for departure. But nothing could prepare me for the terrible feeling of loneliness I experienced as I boarded the aircraft bound for Nairobi, Kenya.

4
Africa

The low droning of the aircraft engine awoke me and for a moment I thought I was dreaming. Outside the window a vast plain of scorching white sand glared in the hot sun and it was then that I remembered I was on a plane bound for Africa. A few hours later we touched down at Nairobi and a new phase in my life was about to begin.

Travelling from Nairobi to Gilgil, where I was to be temporarily stationed, was something of a culture shock. Everywhere cliffs and hills collided with azure sky. It was fantastic to be zooming through the Kenyan countryside, enveloped in hot still air, such a contrast with rainy grey Belfast. However, the blistered landscape soon became a watery plain; within weeks the rainy season was upon us. Parched clay roads were transformed into mud tracks and to keep our army boots clean proved an impossible task.

I detested Gilgil. There was little to do but digging and think of home three thousand miles away. However, the monotony was suddenly broken by the eruption of the Cuban missile crisis. Russia had sent ships to Cuba and Kennedy was threatening to blow them out of the water. Immediately we were put on red alert, expecting at any moment to be flown out to Germany, though it's doubtful what good our conventional weapons would have been against atomic warfare. But the crisis subsided and so did our excitement; we returned to the routine of army life.

A short time after that I said goodbye to Gilgil, much to my relief, and was transferred to work with the 24th field ambulance in Nairobi. This job involved driving medical officers to perform surgery or taking their wives on shopping trips. I enjoyed Nairobi but it was the place which was to be my downfall.

Scouse Webster, Scouse Blake and some other soldiers became my drinking pals and the NAAFI became my home. Most nights I had a glass in my hand. At the weekend we hit the bars and clubs in downtown Nairobi with our hip flasks full of booze at our sides.

Our common interest in alcohol led us to form a club called the Alsops Alcoholics Association (Alsops being the name of the brewery) or the AAA for short. Uniforms of a special shirt, light trousers and sandals made us easily identifiable around camp. The only qualification necessary to join the AAA was a love of 'firewater', and potential members needed to be drunk on a regular basis. Our group was no place for moderate drinkers.

We soon developed a reputation for crazy stunts. Drink gave us the courage to venture into parts of Nairobi out of bounds to troops. We knowingly entered 'trouble' bars, and this resulted in frequent fights. Often the Military Police came bursting in and we ended up in the back of police trucks speeding off to a military guardhouse. The following day we were brought before our Commanding Officer and were charged with being drunk and disorderly. We didn't deliberately go out to fight, but once we had a taste of the hard stuff we were ready for anything. Incidents like this became the norm in my life and those of my mates. The Military Police and the RAF police knew that the AAA spelt trouble.

Most organizations plan trips for their members, perhaps to a nearby town or city to do some sightseeing. Our excursions involved visiting Alsops Breweries. Our association carried their name so this put us in good favour with this particular brewery. Trips involved not so much a tour of the distillery as taking advantage of the abundance of free drink available.

At any given time there was at least one member of the AAA in military prison. I spent several spells being detained at Her Majesty's pleasure. The military prison was situated in an isolated area outside Nairobi and life was thoroughly miserable for its inmates. We were all squeezed into one large billet, and the food was appalling. I loved to whistle, but this was a forbidden pleasure; happiness was kept outside the prison doors.

One particular fierce-looking prison officer took an instant dislike to me. Every morning his booming voice disturbed my sweet dreams.

'Come on, McIlwaine! Get up and get your mates up!' he bellowed, sending shivers down my spine.

For a while I was submissive, but I soon got sick of being the target of this man's insults. One morning I blatantly refused to carry out his wishes; even his threats of bringing me before the CO on a charge of insubordination didn't make me back down. He carried out his threat and I was hauled in front of my commanding officer.

'Well, McIlwaine, what have you got to say for yourself? You are in enough trouble as it is without disobeying orders!'

'Sir, I... feel I'm being picked on by the NCO,' I replied nervously. 'I'd like to bring a charge of discrimination against him.' I couldn't believe that I'd said the words, they'd tumbled out before I'd had a chance to stop them.

The CO looked at me in disbelief.

'Do you understand what you've just said?' he asked abruptly. 'I would advise you to rethink your last statement.'

But I stood my ground. 'I'm sorry, sir, but I don't think I can do that,' I answered firmly.

I couldn't believe that this powerful man was trying to bargain with me and persuade me to change my mind. Although I was eventually going to give in, I felt that if I made him sweat a bit first the charge against me might get dropped. My plan worked! I retracted my statement on the condition that the prison officer stopped harassing me and was let off with a warning.

Although I really hated the prison régime, that didn't prevent me from ending up inside several more times because of drink-related incidents.

One time when I was confined to camp for committing an offence, the frustrations of army life began to overwhelm me. Drinking was no consolation, so I decided I had to get out. I planned to go AWOL— absent without leave. A duty driver gave me a lift to the Mombasa road and from here I planned to stow away on a ship bound for England. Soon I would be back in the real world.

The Mombasa road was a lonely place. I attempted to hitch a ride but was unsuccessful. Darkness descended and brought with it a series of shrieks and cries, a fearsome reminder of the wild animals roaming the area. I was alone and frightened on a strange road in a foreign country. Unable to bear the solitude, I fled back to the safety of the camp, where I scrambled over the barbed wire and dashed back to my room. Later that night a duty corporal questioned me about my whereabouts, but I managed to talk my way out of the situation. This put a stop to my drink-inspired plans to escape from the army and from Africa. I was forced to stay put and serve my time.

For most of us, life in the army was boring and frustrating. Drink was an escape—and a hazard. Once when we were on standby to go to Uganda, our weapons strapped to us day and night, one of our drinking sessions nearly ended in tragedy. One of my mates was fooling around with his Sterling sub-machine-gun in one of the billets when suddenly there was a burst of machine-gun fire across the wall. The safety-catch hadn't been on. At the time we thought this incident was funny and laughed it off, but anyone in the path of that gun could have been killed. We managed to fill in the holes in the wall and get more rounds for the gun, and much to our relief the incident passed unnoticed by the army hierarchy.

One hot steamy night I was out on exercises with Scouse Blake from Birkenhead. As usual we headed for a pub. After a few drinks we lost our inhibitions and began to sing really antagonistic songs, which attracted fierce glares from soldiers from other regiments who were in the bar. We realized that they would tear us apart if we didn't get out, so we made a swift departure and managed to get back to our makeshift camp. After bedding down for the night, we thought little more of the incident and drifted off to sleep. Suddenly I was in a dream where I was being violently beaten; but it wasn't a dream, the soldiers had come to seek revenge. Their shadowy figures towered above me. I began to scream. My wild yells did the trick, and the men bolted, fearing that the sentries would swoop and arrest them.

I can see now that my drinking habits put me in many hazardous situations. At that point in my life I don't think I was an alcoholic. I was still able to carry on my normal daily routine without having a 'fix'. But I was gradually moving from social drinker to alcoholic. Wines and spirits were cheap in East Africa and there was little else for servicemen to do but drink. White girls tended to look down on soldiers, preferring to go out with rich white farmers or bank clerks. I did some horse-riding, and tried archery; anything to fill in time. At that time racial tensions were running high, so we were really restricted to camp. To venture outside could mean death. So our nights were spent within the confines of the camp and when we visited the night-clubs in Nairobi it was always in a group.

While I was in Nairobi I had first-hand experience of the racial conflict. Two RAF men had knocked down an African while out in their jeep in Nairobi. They had stopped to see how badly he was hurt and were immediately attacked by his tribesmen. They were killed and their bodies were badly mutilated. So when I found myself in a similar situation I was in no doubt what to do.

I was returning from a cross-country race, and driving up to the Northern frontier desert to go on exercise. While speeding along a dusty road, a huge Masai warrior, complete with spear and shield, suddenly stepped into my path. I couldn't brake soon enough and, to my horror, I mowed him down. I didn't stop my truck as it was against orders, and when I reached the desert I reported the incident to my sergeant-major. He told me I had acted properly; if I'd stopped I could have been ambushed and killed. It was unfortunate and distressing that we had to take those measures, but that's what the situation called for.

Despite my initial homesickness I can now look back on my three years in Kenya with great fondness. I really grew to love the country. The climate, the landscape, the animals—the whole way of life was something I'll never forget. Scenes such as the stunning Great Rift Valley, the slender giraffes lazing in the sunlight, and snow on the top of Mount Kenya remain with me now—magnificent scenes which are without equal, scenes which a poor boy from Belfast never dreamt existed.

The time came for Britain to grant Kenya her independence and there was a gradual withdrawal of troops. The Kenyans were delighted. They had resented the British presence in their country and were glad to see us go. I was scheduled to leave towards the end of 1964, but before leaving I was given a two-week holiday which I spent soaking up the sun in beautiful Mombasa. A friend and I lazed on a white sandy beach fringed with palm trees, drinking beer. After a day's sunbathing we hit the night-clubs. The whole holiday was one big boozing session.

Soon we were back in Nairobi, where we were informed that in a few days we would be flying back to Britain. Goodbyes were said to friends and colleagues. With a strong sense of sadness I boarded the aircraft bound for England, and Kenya faded into memory.

5

Return

The plane touched down after many hours of hazardous flying. It had been a nightmarish flight. At the stopover in Khartoum we'd drunk as much booze as we could. Then one of the engines had lost power over the Swiss Alps and the jagged peaks seemed almost to touch the shaking plane, ready to slice it in two. I visualized the headlines in Belfast's daily newspapers—'Belfast soldier killed over Swiss Alps'—and with this morbid thought I hit the bottle even harder. The hazy form of Stansted airport could not come soon enough for me and I vowed never to set foot on a plane again.

After spending a week in London, I took the Heysham ferry and headed back home to Belfast. I had been away for three whole years. It was a good feeling to step off the boat and see a throng of familiar faces, waiting to welcome me back.

Wilton Street looked exactly the same; it was as if time had stood still. Happy children played on the pavements; people stood in the icy air, hands in pockets, discussing the price of bread and who was marrying who. Number 98, the place I called home, looked no different—perhaps just a little smaller. Inside was my mother waiting anxiously; the lines were etched more firmly on her face, her hair was a little greyer. Instantly she threw her arms around me, her son had come home.

The news that I'd returned spread round the district like wildfire and I became the star attraction. People were constantly coming to our house to see 'Annie McIlwaine's wee son who had been away in the wilds of Africa'. Then suddenly the people stopped coming, the novelty was over, and it was back to the routine of daily living and the old escapism through the booze. Lizzie Thompson's pub became my regular haunt and each drinking session ended with me being carried home legless. Gambling was another of my favourite pastimes; I blew a lot of money on horses that never came in. My mother noticed the change in my life— 'One boy went to Africa, a different one came back,' she said.

Before leaving Africa I had chosen a posting in Germany. But this did not come off and I ended up spending the remainder of my military service at Army Headquarters at Thiepval Barracks, Lisburn, Northern Ireland as part of the 26th Company of the Royal Corps of Transport. This was poles apart from driving Land Rovers in the wilds of Africa. Three-ton trucks became the order of the day and my job was very much that of a glorified taxi-driver. The Sperrin Mountains, near Ballymena, became the new terrain. We ferried recruits up there to go on exercises.

I remember one particular trip to the Royal Ulster Rifles Training Depot in Ballymena. After taking some recruits there for manoeuvres, I was informed I had to stay overnight, confined to camp. I was dying to get out of the stuffy atmosphere to have some fun, but I was in army uniform and had no civilian clothes with me.

'I wanna get out of this place, maybe go to the Flamingo Ballroom. You couldn't lend me a suit or something could you?' I asked a young recruit.

He agreed, but he was smaller than me and once dressed in his suit I looked like Norman Wisdom!

Undeterred by my ridiculous appearance, however, I headed off to the pub to get drunk before going to the dance. But once I got to the Flamingo and saw all the sharply-dressed guys, I felt foolish and went back to the pub for more booze. Most of the camp probably heard my boisterous return. My shouts and yells brought the orderly officer on the scene and he escorted me to the guardroom.

'You've no right to put me in here,' I snarled. 'I don't even belong to this camp, I'm just here on manoeuvres!'

'While you're in the camp you're under our jurisdiction,' he replied. 'I'll let you go this one time, McIlwaine, but step out of line one more time and you'll go into the slammer!'

So I managed to escape serious trouble and was ordered to go to bed. The following morning the heavy steps of the duty corporal signalled that it was time to get up. After harassing the young recruits he approached my bed, grabbed my legs and ordered me out of bed.

'Who do you think you're talking to?' I shouted. 'I'm not a recruit, you can't order me around!'

My arrogance again landed me in trouble and again I was almost put on charge. I was always running into trouble.

Later that day, after dropping the recruits off in the Sperrin Mountains, several drivers including myself headed back to Army HQ in Lisburn. We decided to break the journey by stopping at a roadside pub and as usual I came out tipsy. I climbed into my truck, started the engine and reversed straight into the front of a car. Luckily my vehicle escaped damage, but the car was slightly dented. However, I decided not to hang around for the consequences, and took off immediately. I knew that the police would be brought in and that I could face a charge of drunken driving. I was not prepared for that.

A few months later I travelled up to Broughshane, a small village outside Ballymena, to deliver a truck-load of bread to troops on exercises. When I arrived they appeared to have sufficient supplies and refused to accept the delivery. But one of the officers signed for it and told me to dispose of it whatever way I wanted. This seemed to be a great opportunity to make some money, so I returned to Belfast and began to sell the bread to shopkeepers on the Shankill Road. I made quite a lot of cash, but most of it ended up in the till at the local pub.

During my time at Thieval Barracks I was chosen to be part of a guard of honour for a visiting general. My attitude was totally anti-establishment, and I was determined that there was no way that I was going to co-operate. I made excuses, tried to play sick, did everything I could to get out of it, but nothing worked and I found myself having to take part in rehearsals. During the practice there was a shout of 'Call out the guard.' All the troops had to run out into the courtyard for the general salute. That is, all the troops except me: I didn't move. I sat totally apathetic and nonchalant with it. As I expected, the sergeant-major soon appeared on the scene.

'What do you think you're playing at, Driver McIlwaine?' he roared.

'I'm sorry, sir. There's no way I'm taking part in this rehearsal,' I said.

Now the sergeant-major was really seething.

'If you don't take part, I'll lock you up and throw away the key!' he shouted.

These scare tactics did not move me, however, and I refused adamantly to move. The guards were called back into the room and I was ordered to run out with the rest of them after the shout. Once more the shout came: 'Call out the guard.' But again I didn't move.

The furious sergeant-major carried out his threat and I was dragged off and thrown into a cell. Within ten minutes one of the other officers came and tried to sweet-talk me, but I didn't break. After a visit to the CO I reluctantly agreed to take part in the guard of honour.

This is just one example of my persistent defiance of the army and all that it stood for. I seemed to be in constant trouble and clashed continually with the hierarchy. Much of this defiance must have stemmed from the booze. My big mouth landed me in many fights and punch-ups. My rebellious attitude must have been a real headache for the officers.

They say that when a man is drunk he loses control of his actions. That was certainly true in my case. One Saturday night I was sitting drinking in a Lisburn pub. The table was cluttered with empty glasses and I was pretty intoxicated. Out of the corner of my eye I saw a large, ruddy-faced man staring at me intently. Immediately I challenged him and soon we were involved in a full-scale argument. Our words became more and more heated until suddenly his fist was in my eye. I fell to the ground, my hand over my throbbing face. The fight had developed over something trivial— and this was not the only occasion I got hurt.

Tom Quinn and Jimmy Reynolds were my favourite boozing pals at this time and when I was off duty we used to hit dances held in chapels around the Ardoyne, a Republican area of Belfast. The fact that these social gatherings were held in Catholic parochial halls didn't bother me at the time. I had numbered Catholics among my army friends. However, one night we walked up the Falls Road, which was predominantly Republican, singing 'The Sash', a Protestant party song. It's a miracle that we lived to tell the tale, because to act in such an antagonistic way was to invite violence. I suppose it was just one of many silly and dangerous episodes that alcohol inspired.

The hot summer of 1965 brought with it the annual Loyalist celebration held on the twelfth of July and commonly known just as 'the Twelfth'. Twelfth fever was running high; and I was instantly caught up in the frenzy, having been away for three years. On the eve of the parade I invited a couple of my army friends from Scotland and England to come up to my house on the Shankill Road. We partied for most of the night. After a while my Scottish friend announced he was going back to the barracks, but Bob (my friend from England) and I continued drinking and said we would return in the morning.

Bleary-eyed and with hangovers, we set off the following day for Victoria Street Railway Station to catch a train to Lisburn. On the way we decided to stop in an area called Sandy Row for a quick drink and to watch the parade pass through. But one drink led to another and then another and soon we were back to our state of the previous night. Somehow I got separated from Bob and drifted off to see the parade. The rest of that day is a blur.

I found myself on a train to Army HQ but got off before it reached Lisburn. I ended up back in Sandy Row, penniless, and was forced to make the long trek across Belfast to get to the Shankill Road. Yet again I was in trouble. I was absent without leave, much to my mother's distress. When I got back to barracks I pleaded guilty and fortunately got off with a fine.

My army career was chequered to say the least. By this time I had become thoroughly disillusioned with army life. After talking to a Scottish friend I decided I wanted out. Jock had put it so clearly.

'You know, Billy,' he said. 'I'm fed up with this job. We're not really serving our country, we're more like glorified taxi-drivers than soldiers. I'm getting out!'

The more I thought about it, the more I agreed with Jock. And the more I liked his plan. But it was going to be a difficult stunt to pull off. After all, I had signed nine years of my life away to Her Majesty's Forces. I watched Jock carefully. He began to play sick all the time and told the CO he had mental problems and needed to see a shrink. He obviously put on a convincing act because his little scheme worked. But when I tried to pull off the same stunt it was a disaster.

When Jock was admitted to hospital suffering from ulcers, I was surprised to find his sickness was for real. It occurred to me that I too might have developed an ulcer and so the medical officer sent me over to the Musgrave Park Hospital Military Wing for tests. The results showed that I actually did have a duodenal ulcer and I was kept in hospital for treatment. This ulcer neatly put an end to my military service and, much to my relief, I was given a medical discharge. My army career was over.

6

Drinking and Sinking

A click of the letter-box and I raced into the hallway. Sometimes junk mail was strewn over the floor, but occasionally I was rewarded with a small white envelope bearing a USA stamp: another letter from Sally.

We had been writing to each other since I'd been in Africa. She was also from Belfast, but living in America. Our long-distance friendship began when Sally befriended my sister Margaret and they moved into an apartment together in the States. Despite the oceans separating us we developed a close relationship and when Sally came home on holiday, romance bloomed. We decided to marry.

Sally wanted me to join her in the States, but I was reluctant. We were constantly being confronted with violent images of America on our television screens. That worried me. Little did I know what Belfast would turn out to be.

It was Christmas Eve 1965. I waited anxiously in the arrivals lounge of Dublin Airport for the flight which would bring Margaret and Sally home. Members of both families had gathered to welcome them back from the States. They were coming home for good. Later that day Sally and I got officially engaged.

'You know that I like a drink, don't you Sally?' I asked nervously. 'If you marry me you have to accept this.'

Even then I knew that my life was becoming more

and more dependent on alcohol and it was starting to become a crutch. The drinking had not stopped after my discharge from the army: if anything it had got worse. I had begun working on the night-shift in James Mackie and Sons, a local engineering factory. I was based in the stud shop, making components for textile machinery, and I enjoyed the freedom of being an ordinary civilian again.

My days were divided between work and drinking. Many times I walked into Mackie's tipsy, having stopped at one of the local pubs on the way to work. On dry nights I slipped under the heavy tarpaulins covering the huge iron skids located out in the yard for finishing jobs. Usually after an hour or so asleep I was sober enough to go back to work. My workmates and I covered for each other if the supervisors asked any questions.

Sally knew about my drinking, but she was still prepared to marry me. Throughout 1966 we made preparations for the big day. Things were going well. Sally got a job in a local tobacco factory and we were able to buy a small but comfortable house on the Shankill Road. But one evening, a few weeks before the wedding day, a hot and furious argument erupted. In the barrage of shouting we both said it was over, the engagement was off!

I missed Sally like mad, but neither of us, in our stubborn pride, would do anything to bring reconciliation. One Saturday evening I had a visit from my sister Clara and her husband, Charlie.

'Billy, we're going out for a drink, will you come with us?' Clara asked.

'Thanks, but I'm not very good company at the minute, Clara. You two go ahead, I'll be OK,' I said, in a resigned, weary manner.

But my reply wasn't good enough for Clara. 'Look,

you're just sitting around here moping,' she said. 'We're taking you out, so go and get your coat on!'

Finally I gave in to my sister and went with them to the local pub. Unknown to me, Clara and Charlie had also been to see Sally and had asked her out for a drink. Suddenly, at the bar, we were confronted with each other. The old pride still kept us apart and we refused to sit together. But as the evening wore on Clara and Charlie managed to talk us into a reconciliation. We got our problems ironed out and the wedding was on again.

My sister Anne had recently married and Sally and I began to spend quite a bit of time with her and her husband, Frank. At the weekends he and I hit the local pubs and usually returned home drunk, much to my sister's annoyance. Frank didn't drink much when left to himself and so she felt I was a bad influence. This was largely true. By that time I was drinking so much myself that I wanted other people to do the same in order to justify it.

The countdown to our wedding was almost at an end. I remember going to Burton's with my brother Charlie, who was to be my best man, to buy the wedding suits. We were going to pay for them on the HP. It would be a lot of money to repay—but the Hire Purchase agreement stretched away into the future.

Later that day we were sitting in a pub and Charlie was scanning the racing section of the local paper.

'Hey, Billy, look at the odds against this horse,' he said. 'It's a cert to win! Why don't we have a little flutter?'

'But we haven't a shilling between us,' I replied. Then I began to think about the money we could make, money I could use for booze. 'Unless well... maybe we could put the suits in the pawn and take them out when the horse wins.'

Unfortunately our hot tip didn't live up to our expectations and the horse came in fifth. Somehow we managed to retrieve the outfits, but it underlined the fact that I was willing to put my wedding plans in jeopardy just to have money for drink.

Sally and I finally tied the knot on 17th September 1966 at the North Belfast Mission. The wedding was a small affair. Afterwards we spent a week at my sister's caravan in a picturesque village called Groomsport. Not long after we arrived I took Sally to the local pub: she got sick, not being used to drinking; I got drunk. A great start to our married life!

A week later we returned to Belfast and to normality. I began working nine-to-five in Mackie's and decided to take on a second job at night. One of my favourite pubs was the Star Bar, and I soon became friends with the owner, Billy Beggs. One night he approached me with a proposition.

'How would you feel about becoming a more permanent fixture here, Billy?' he asked. 'There's a job goin'. Are you interested?'

'Well, I need more time to think about it, and I need to talk it over with Sally,' I replied.

The more I thought about it, the more the idea appealed to me. I would have the perfect reason for being in the pub: I would be on official business, but could still enjoy a good drink. Of course I didn't say this to Sally; instead I emphasized the benefits of the extra money it would bring in. She agreed and so I took the job. I was to be constantly surrounded by my poison.

Brewery trips were important days in the pub calendar. Usually we were taken around the plant to watch how various drinks were made, but I was more interested in the free booze afterwards than the scientific methods used to produce it.

I remember going to a brewery on Belfast's Glen

Road with Tony Logan, a colleague of mine. After a quick dash round the brewery we headed for the reception, where we were told that unlimited free booze was available. This was like putting a child in a sweet-shop; we went berserk. I returned home extremely drunk. Sally was absolutely disgusted. She was beginning to see that she had married a man who was a drinker much worse than she could ever have imagined.

Another trip was organized, this time to McArdles Brewery in Dundalk. Again, I ended up totally stoned. Indeed, these visits were really only boozing parties. Working in the bar wasn't helping me at all: it was making me worse. Each night after closing time we cleaned up the lounge and were allowed a staff drink. After that we bought a few rounds for each other and then I staggered home around midnight, or one in the morning. At this point I was beginning to cross the line from social drinker to alcoholic.

Not long after I started working in the Star Bar I noticed a group of men, five friends who came in regularly. Many nights Bertie Ewing, Harry Clark, Johnny Porter, Jimmy Quinn and Ernie Weir drank and lingered over tense games of dominoes. One night they asked me to join them for a drink and that was the beginning of a close relationship which lasted many years. All these men were hard drinkers, which suited me. At weekends Sally joined me at the bar, and they also brought their wives. Together we went out to many functions—the women enjoyed the dancing, the men enjoyed the booze.

By now I was hitting the bottle harder and harder. At every opportunity I was propping up the bar. After work I used to spend a few hours drinking and then tell Sally I'd been working overtime. Then I got to the point where I wanted—I *needed*—to have alcohol close to me all the time. I started to hide bottles of porter among the piles of glistening black coal in the bunker in our back yard. I hoped Sally would not find them. Then, when I couldn't get to the pub, I would crack them open.

I needed the assurance of alcohol. The eight-hour dry stretch at work began to be torture. I solved the problem by putting a couple of bottles of porter in the locker beside my machine. When I needed a drink I strapped a bottle inside my belt under my overall for drinking in the toilet. Drinking on the job was risky, so I killed the pungent smell with a swig of cough medicine.

One icy December morning I had a strong craving for drink. I threw open my locker—empty, except for an old pair of boots. Beads of sweat formed on my forehead. I was panic-stricken.

'Oh, God,' I thought, 'I need a drink!'

I desperately needed that warm secure feeling. Within seconds I was approaching the foreman. I had to think of some excuse to get out of the factory for a few minutes.

'Ah... I'm not feeling too good, I um... need to go to first aid,' I lied.

To my relief the foreman was taken in by my little act and gave me a pass to visit the medical station. I rushed out past the huge iron factory gates on to the Springfield Road. I walked straight past the gate leading to first aid—the aid I needed was the alcoholic kind. I headed for the nearest pub, and after two or three pints my frenzy subsided. Alcoholism was taking its toll.

Never a week went by when I received full pay. Spending afternoons slumped over a table of empty glasses, instead of being at work, became habitual. I joined a darts club in the Wellington Bar, and loud smoky pubs became my natural habitat. There was something about a pub. I told myself it was because in a pub I could be myself. In reality I was sinking and sinking and not coming up for air.

One morning I woke up with a worse than usual hangover—it had been a rough night. Despite my pounding head and lurching stomach I got dressed for work, but made sure I had a drink before I left. I thought this would help quell the sickness. But by mid-morning I still felt rotten, as I stood tightly gripping my machine, trying to steady myself, trying to hold on to reality. The never-ceasing warring sound was shooting through my brain, but suddenly the noise changed... I was at a race course, the pounding of hoofs on turf, the sharp rhythm of commentators' voices were swimming through my head. I covered my ears, trying to blot out the fury inside my brain. I had to get out!

'Once I'm out in the air I'll feel better,' I told myself.

But even after half an hour of pacing the yard, the voices still tormented me. Once again I went to see the foreman.

'I'm feeling really sick, I need to go home for a while,' I stuttered.

He looked at me in disbelief.

'Look, McIlwaine, you had better knuckle down to some work or you'll be getting your cards!'

But then he must have noticed my ghost-like face, because he suddenly said, 'OK, this once you can go.'

I staggered out of work and into the nearest pub. The alcohol crushed the voices until they became only a whisper. Finally the war of noise stopped—silence. Silence, that is, until another frenzy started within my body. My heart started to pump erratically. I thought it was going to explode out of my chest! It was uncontrollable, and I thought I was dying. Looking back, I realize I was probably on the verge of a nervous breakdown.

Terrified, I called a taxi and went home. Sally was there and I began to open up to her.

'I feel so bad. I know I'm hooked on the drink. What am I going to do?'

'You've got to fight it, break its hold on you,' Sally urged me.

But, despite my wife's positive words, by then I was entrenched, totally trapped within a vicious circle. A circle from which there seemed no escape.

The expense of the drink was crippling. Before long I began to get involved with money-lenders. But once I had the cash in my hand, I gave little thought as to how I would pay it back and meet the high interest rates. I could only think in the short term: the money would buy me drink and temporary security. Soon my wallet would be empty and I would crawl back to the money-lenders once more. Caught in a spiral of debt, I was forced to hide from certain people or face the consequences. Sometimes if I was desperate for money I raced to get home from work on a Friday night before Sally, and grabbed a suit or watch to pawn. I steered clear of the local pawnbrokers and headed for the Falls Road where nobody knew me. I also spent many hours in the bookie's waiting for the 'big win' that would wipe away all my financial problems. But at the end of the week my wallet was frequently empty and I had no money to give to Sally, only a barrage of excuses.

I spent long nights awake, gazing at the shadowy bedroom walls, wracking my brains for money-making schemes. Deception ruled my life and my relationships. I was well on the way down the slippery slope.

7

Religion No Barricade

The year 1969 plunged Northern Ireland into a kind of religious apartheid. Suddenly I was torn away from close friends and relatives because it suited the politics of the powerful. Over the years I had formed a close friendship with my brother-in-law, Frank. The fact that he was a Catholic didn't matter to me; religious bigotry was not a problem at the time. I very happily drank in predominantly Republican areas such as the Markets and the Falls Road. Every Saturday, Frank and I went on our weekly drinking spree, sometimes in his area, sometimes mine. We got to know each other's friends, they knew we were from 'the other side' and accepted it.

At that time there was generally a spirit of goodwill between Protestants and Catholics. The old myths and bitterness were starting to break down and were being replaced by integration. Each Saturday saw a throng of shoppers from the Falls Road crossing over to the Shankill to hunt for bargains. Protestants had no hesitation in having a few pints in the pubs on the Falls Road. On football weekends a long line of supporters snaked its way down the Falls Road and into Micky Hammil's and Dan Finnegan's for a few pints before the match.

I think our common backgrounds brought us together. We worshipped in different churches, but both faced the same daily struggles to survive. Money was as scarce on the Shankill as it was on the Falls; there were few rich people in either area. This bond seemed to cut across the religious and political divide. I myself could never identify with the Unionist politics associated with my area. The 'fur coat brigade', as they came to be called, were poles apart from the harsh realities of life on the Shankill, and in my opinion only used working-class Protestants to put them into power.

Mixed marriages had become more common, drawing families from across the divide closer together. In the sixties people were able to visit friends in other areas without fear and intimidation—that is, until that fateful day in August 1969, which changed people's lives and the course of history for ever. I often thought that before the outbreak of the Troubles Protestants and Catholics were getting on too well, disturbing certain elements in society who had other aspirations. When these individuals saw that people like Frank and me could go out together as friends it bothered them; they wanted to sever those bonds and divide society.

And they were successful. Once the violence erupted, my brother-in-law could no longer come over to the Star Bar; his religion alone made him a prime target for gunmen. I couldn't vouch for his life, so our relationship came to a standstill. I was unwilling to venture into his area for the same fate almost certainly awaited me. I knew the Provisional IRA would have no hesitation in shooting me. We were family, lived in the same city, and yet we might as well have lived at opposite ends of the world.

Bombs and bullets became part of our reality, and to be in the wrong place at the wrong time spelled danger and even death. This was the fate of a friend of mine. Benny Tate was a representative for one of the alcohol companies and was Catholic. Despite the obvious danger, he continued to come to the bars on the Shankill Road. One afternoon, several gunmen burst into a bar, grabbed him and bundled him into a waiting car. Half an hour later he lay dead at the foot of the Knockagh Monument outside Belfast, a stream of blood trickling from his head. This was just one of a spate of tragedies perpetrated by those who wanted to destroy any kind of peace or normality.

The summer of 1969 was hot in more ways than one. The air was heavy with tension, uncertainty pervaded the atmosphere. Events were coming to a head and very soon would explode, hurling Belfast into the news headlines all over the world. I was still working in the Star Bar and a few months earlier had been appointed Chairman of the Social Club. We had decided that our members needed to get out of the city; they needed a change of scene. So the committee members and I had organized a trip to Blackrock, a small town in Southern Ireland. But, on the eve of our excursion, serious rioting broke out on the Shankill and the road was strewn with bottles and bricks and several people were injured. Some of the social club's officers were concerned about our trip because of the tension in the area.

'Look, I think we should go,' I said to the officers. 'We've made all the arrangements, the bus is paid for and, as well as that, the people need to get away from this road for a few hours.'

Early the next morning the bus arrived and we felt we should leave as planned. A few hours later we reached Blackrock and straight away my mates and I headed for the nearest pub. We really were not interested in seeing the town, all we wanted to see was the inside of the town's bars. Once we had some 'firewater' inside us we were ready for a singsong, and of course we threw a few party songs into our repertoire. After the strains of 'The Sash' the locals realized we were from the North. News of the riots in Belfast had travelled south and so we began to attract angry glares.

Someone began to belt out the 'Soldier's Song' and the rest of the crowd joined in, showing their support for Northern Irish Catholics. As we tried to drown one another out in song, the atmosphere became more and more heated and we left the pub in a hurry before serious fighting erupted.

Half an hour later we were in Dundalk. After our group had been given the customary lecture on time of departure, most of the women headed for the shops to look for some last-minute bargains. Bertie Ewing and I felt another drinking session was called for. As pint followed pint we totally lost track of time. Soon Davy McMullan was on the scene.

'Come on, you two. The bus is waiting! Finish up your drinks!'

But while he was waiting for us he decided to order a pint. We finally made it back to the bus to be confronted with a group of very angry people.

'Where have you been?' one elderly woman shouted. 'You tell us to be back at a certain time and then you come back one hour later. What a great example you are!'

The journey back to Belfast was a quiet one. The jovial atmosphere which had marked our outward trip had gone. As we neared the grey mass of Belfast city centre, anxiety was clearly written on every face. No one knew what kind of situation we were returning to.

As we drove up the Shankill the area seemed to be enveloped in a kind of hush, as if it were holding its breath. Before long we heard frenzied shouting. We knew we were in trouble. A crowd was attacking a huddled group of B Specials. As our bus moved towards the multitude, a wave of panic came over the passengers. By this time, the news of our trip to Southern Ireland had become common knowledge. As feelings were running high against Southerners, we were branded as traitors and youths were threatening to stone our bus. Swiftly we pushed everyone out of the bus, while the B Specials struggled to control the surging throng. Much to our relief, everyone got home safely but shaken.

That night Sally took our daughter Rhonda, who had been born the previous November, to her sister's house in another part of Belfast, but I stayed. As Bertie Ewing and I walked up the Shankill, it was hard to believe our eyes. The pavement was covered with glass and shops had been looted by hordes of youths. Seeing all this made me totally ashamed to be called a Protestant. These rioters were wrecking and pillaging their own area.

In the aftermath accusations were hurled at Catholics from the Falls Road. Eyewitnesses said that they had been seen running up the Cashmir Road with all types of stolen goods. But I know what I saw. I was sickened by the thought that we had been branded as traitors for a day trip into Southern Ireland, when the very people who considered themselves to be good Protestants and Loyalists were destroying their own district and getting away with it.

8

Nightmare Unleashed

The vicious street violence that swept through the community in those early days of the Troubles has now faded into memory. Many people are too young to remember, but those that do can testify that it changed their lives. From that time onward, people were forced to adapt to a new environment of brick-strewn roads, gunfire, bombed buildings, dead friends and relatives. For many the emotional turbulence was too much: they turned to the bottle.

There were no such things as closing hours in the pubs in those days. Law and order had broken down, so pub owners worried little about police raids. In almost any community you could find at least one place open in the small hours of the morning. A knock at the side door was all that was needed to enter, usually to find a room jam-packed with people, heavy with the stench of alcohol and smoke. When people were so drunk and tired that they couldn't take any more, they went home.

During the chaotic atmosphere of 1969 there was a spate of pub fires. Owners were intimidated into leaving premises, crates of alcohol were carried out and buildings were set alight. Looting of pubs was a frequent occurrence, so there was no shortage of drink. Alcohol was freely available and for many it seemed to offer instant escape, and so they were sucked into its power.

The early violence in Belfast had little romanticism or excitement about it. It was bloody and extremely frightening. To be in the midst of a sea of flying bricks, tear-gas and gunfire, where confusion reigns and hatred pervades the atmosphere, is a harrowing experience. Alcohol became a way of forgetting the horror, gaining peace and, at the same time, courage to return to the fight and do your part. The old 'firewater' was true to its name and so in the breaks from the fighting many people returned to their local pubs, to bury their faces in beer glasses. Without alcohol I felt insecure, inadequate and very much afraid.

Nobody wants to be looked on as a coward—we all want to be in control. The booze helped me to talk big and think big. Once that warm liquid was inside me I could go anywhere and challenge anyone. What I didn't recognize was that the effect was temporary and totally artificial. Strip a man of the bottle and he's stammering, nervous—he's nothing. I became dependent on drink because I wanted people to see me as a strong courageous person, not to see the real, frightened me.

In the midst of all the turmoil, alcohol became a definite form of escapism and certain people began to take advantage of the situation. The paramilitary organizations which had sprung up wanted to defend the areas in which they lived and needed money to do so. Their leaders, seeing the market for booze, decided that was where the money lay. They began to take over derelict houses and commercial properties all over Belfast and, after obtaining supplies of booze from secret sources, illegal shibeens went into full swing. To win customers they made their alcohol cheaper than the pubs. People flocked in and some spent more time in these clubs than in their own homes. The shibeens hummed with money-making activities: whether it was card schools or one-armed bandits, most of the proceeds went into the kitty of the paramilitaries.

Many communities at the time were steeped in alcohol. People who had previously had a drink just a few times a week now found themselves being offered drink from every direction and found it difficult to refuse. In these circumstances I became a person totally absorbed in and addicted to alcohol. As we drifted into the seventies the number of deaths jumped from double to triple figures; but the faceless people in the statistics were someone's husband, someone's sister, someone's friend. They were robbed of their lives, leaving behind a community torn apart by grief. Seeing death and destruction every day plays havoc with the emotions. I couldn't cope with the realities of everyday life without a solace.

Sometimes it was difficult to believe that this was the city in which I had grown up. Belfast had had a tremendous community spirit. I remembered how newspaper headlines in my childhood, recording murder and violence in England, had affected me. I had been thankful that I lived in Northern Ireland, where those things were virtually unknown. But now things had totally changed. It seemed like a nightmare that the people of the city I loved could turn into such monsters. Although I didn't believe in God or any sort of higher power at the time, I felt strongly that when those first few bombs had gone off, those first few shots had been fired, thousands of demons had been unleashed. The men of violence had become Satan's instruments and were continually stooping to new depths of evil. Then the use of torture began to creep into the conflict. When a member of one community captured an opponent, it became not just a matter of shooting them, but of subjecting them to nightmarish agony beforehand. I remember seeing a horrific photograph of a man who had been captured by the provisional IRA. His charred and mutilated body cut into my heart. He had been burnt all over with cigarettes and his thigh cut off with a hatchet; all this probably happened before they finally killed him. I wondered what had became of our society in Northern Ireland? Where had we gone wrong? I couldn't find any answers.

I still spent a lot of time in the Star Bar. It was like a haven from the storm. Despite the horrors which surrounded us, the bar managed to keep its jovial atmosphere and I could sit and chat with friends as if nothing was going on. I could lose myself in drink and talk, blocking out the realities of life.

One Saturday afternoon in 1971 I was slouched along those familiar leather seats and was just about to lift my drink, when a massive explosion went off behind me. The whole place shook and a wave of shock ripped through my body. Seconds before people had been sitting around tables relaxing. Now they were running around frantically, not knowing what to do or where to go. As we all surged outside, we immediately saw that the target of the attack was a large furniture showroom about one hundred yards away. It had been completely flattened by the explosion, reduced to a pile of bricks and rubble. Within a few minutes crowds had gathered, totally stunned by what had happened. Then came the familiar sirens of the emergency services, called out yet again to deal with the aftermath of the terror, all in a day's work.

Everyone who had been in the showroom seemed to be accounted for. Everyone, that is, except for two young babies. When the word spread around the crowd, we all instinctively began to dig with our fingers in the rubble, hoping that somehow we could save them, but knowing deep down it was impossible.

They could not possibly have survived such an explosion. The army diggers were soon on the scene, their huge metal jaws clutching the rubble. After several minutes, a small pale object was uncovered; it was a little child's arm. There are no words to describe the emotional impact of a sight like this. Even the most hardened person could not help but be affected. A group of soldiers nearby had to turn their heads away. Their military training did not equip them for this sort of thing.

'Oh, my God. What is this all about?' I said to myself. Ten minutes before, those little children had been lying in the safety of their prams. And then, suddenly, ruthless terrorists with no regard for human life plunged them into death. I thought of the heartbreak of their mothers, losing their children like that. Their grief did not concern those who planted the deadly bomb. Where was the justification in all this?

I again returned to the Star Bar and buried myself in drink; there was nothing else to do. It seemed that, with a million questions and no answers, the best thing was to lift a glass of whisky and forget about it.

9
Frustration

When the rioting erupted in 1969 no one dreamed that twenty years later Northern Ireland would still be locked in violence. Always there was a feeling that any day someone would come up with a solution and the country would return to normality. After all, the British Government had been involved in wars for hundreds of years. They were intelligent; surely they could find an answer and bring both sides together.

But such positive thinking never became any more than that. For a little while it gave a sense of hope, but no concrete answers were forthcoming. So, as the Troubles began to stretch from year to year, frustration began to mount within me. Meetings were arranged between church leaders and politicians and suddenly our hopes went up, a breakthrough seemed imminent. But after hours of talks no compromise was reached, the leaders were too entrenched in their principles to come to agreement. The venture was a flop.

Internment, imprisonment without trial, was seen to be the salvation of the country. It was hoped that soon the men of violence would be behind bars. But, instead of limiting the violence, this only increased tension and strengthened the determination of the terrorists. Although the leadership was interned, there was never a shortage of people to take their places.

When initiative after initiative flounders, sheer desperation and frustration result. The British Government tried to accommodate minority grievances about jobs, voting and housing, but this did not work. The violence continued to escalate. When a man, woman or child was killed it was a seven days' wonder. For a few days a death was headline news, but then the name and event faded into memory as yet another senseless killing took place. I asked myself, 'How can this be brought to an end? What can I do to stop it?'

One Tuesday night I wandered into a club, edged myself on to a tall leather stool and ordered a drink. The next thing I knew, it was Thursday. A hazy world of faces kept swimming past, staring at me, asking me how I felt, telling me to go home. But I was home, a glass in my hand was all the family I needed.

Sometime on that Thursday, I suddenly found myself staring into the faces of my real family. My wife's pale face was taut with grief. My sister stood close beside her. They were shocked to find me: they thought I had been shot. For three days I had been a ghost, enveloped in a dream world. Once again it was time to face the cold light of day.

10

The Master

From the moment I had crowned alcohol king, my life was not my own. The demon drink ruled over everything. It had conquered my mind and was now conquering my body. I couldn't live without it. But the alcohol was not only attacking me; other people were also being hurt. My relationship with my wife Sally was anything but good. She was sick of a man who was married to booze, who had little commitment to his family and was never at home.

What Sally didn't know was that I couldn't stay at home. I just couldn't see any purpose in it. How could you have a family life, how could you relax, when all around you your country was being torn apart? When I did stay at home, I sat in silence with my lips tightly pursed. I had nothing to talk about. Our way of life was under threat and no one could stop it, so what was there to talk about?

I looked for answers in the pub. Every night a different wise man waved his magic wand of solutions and promised peace. Nothing ever came of all this but I thought I'd keep on listening just in case. Being in the pub gave me a sense of hope: at home there was nothing but depression and the humdrum routine of ordinary life. I had to escape from reality. I didn't know who the next victim of the terrorists would be. I didn't know if I myself would see another day. At that time I was unable to understand why Sally couldn't see that finding a solution had to be my main priority. But I was searching for answers in alcohol, answers that did not exist.

The booze was poisoning my mind and my morality. My most pressing daily concern was to have a couple of crisp pound notes in my wallet—the ticket to a few hours of peace. An empty wallet meant that I had to dream up new schemes and plans. I was prepared to do anything to get alcohol. Suits, coats, watches and rings disappeared into the pawn-shop window. Then they disappeared for good, as I began to get more and more desperate. Soon I ran out of things to pawn, but this did not quell my intense craving for drink. I had to have it, no matter what I had to do. My little daughter's money box, full of shiny pennies she had earnestly saved, became a target for my greedy fingers. Totally ruled by my evil desires, I started to dip my hands into my wife's purse. Soon she was wise to my schemes and carried it with her everywhere.

Now I was forced to look to new sources of money. I decided I might be able to trick the bank into giving me a loan. So one Monday morning I put on the most decent clothes I had and paid my bank a visit. After I had explained that I wanted to buy a new house, my bank manager agreed to lend me six hundred pounds. I was becoming a very good actor. I had no scruples about deception. Six hundred pounds would keep me supplied with alcohol for a while, and to me that was all that mattered. Once I got the money in my hands, I didn't want to know the bank. Their demanding letters didn't scare me until finally they took me to court. By now I was up to my eyes in debt.

So the search went on for that elusive material I thought could buy me happiness.

It was a wet, windy night and I struggled to see out of the misted-up windscreen. The radio was blaring as I had turned up the music to try to keep myself alert. The past few hours had been spent in the Bayardo Bar. Now I was returning home. Just ahead were shadowy figures with reed-like guns by their sides. They signalled me to halt, so I stopped the car and rolled down the window. The fresh-looking face of a young British soldier confronted me.

'Would you mind stepping outside, sir. We want to search your car,' he said.

Reluctantly I got out of the car into the pouring rain. The soldiers were looking for explosives, but all they found in my boot were some bottles of whisky. I carried alcohol with me everywhere.

That night when the soldiers found the booze stashed in the boot, I offered them a drink to try to appease them. But they refused. At that point, out of the corner of my eye, I noticed two men I knew standing across the road. They were brawling. I raced across the street.

'Look, you two, stop this nonsense!' I shouted, trying to pull them apart.

One of the men lifted his bloody face and grabbed me by my collar.

'What business is it of yours? Clear off, McIlwaine. You're not wanted here!' he bellowed.

I took the hint and went back to my car. Within seconds I saw, in my rear-view mirror, a police Land Rover pulling up. A cop poked his head through the window and told me to get out of the car.

'Not again,' I thought.

'We have reason to believe that you're intoxicated, sir,' said the policeman.

'What are you talking about? I'm not drunk!' I protested.

'Look, I can smell it on your breath,' the cop replied in an icy tone. 'We want you to accompany us to the station for some tests. No arguments about it, OK?'

'I told you, I'm not drunk. I don't need tests,' I shouted, as I stepped out of the car.

The policeman put his hand firmly on my shoulder and pointed me in the direction of the Land Rover. Still protesting, I stepped inside and we sped off towards Town Hall Street Police Station.

I was shown into a tiny matchbox of a room, extremely claustrophobic once the door was shut. A police sergeant sat, hands clasped, staring at me from across the table. After being put through the third degree, I was sent to the police doctor. First he told me to walk along a white line and then he told me that he needed a blood sample. I was determined not to co-operate.

'No way. I'm not going to give any blood!' I yelled. 'I'm under no compulsion to give you a sample, OK? I know my rights.'

Once again I found myself in the grey confines of the cell. A cop came in and told me that if I co-operated I could go home. Still I wouldn't give in, but neither would the cop. He continued to persuade me until finally I relented, pulled up my sleeve and let them have a blood sample. The analysis showed that the alcohol level in my blood was well over the limit. I was in big trouble. I knew that my driving licence was in jeopardy.

My court case was scheduled a few weeks later. I knew I needed a drink before I faced a sour-faced old magistrate, so on the morning of my trial I stopped at the Baker's Club in the centre of Belfast for a few quick pints. I left the club half drunk. When I reached the court, I learned to my horror that my case had already been tried and I had been found guilty and stripped of my driving licence for one year. I barged into the wooden-panelled courtroom.

'Who do you think you are?' I shouted at the magistrate. 'You decided my case before I could even defend myself!'

The magistrate gave me an icy stare and then spoke to several police officers standing behind me.

'If you don't get this man out of this court, I'll charge him with disorderly behaviour and throw him in gaol!'

I thought I'd been treated unfairly and decided to stand my ground. But my solicitor appeared and advised me to leave.

'This judge means what he says, Mr McIlwaine. I feel that you should accept that you lost your case and go.'

Reluctantly I marched out of the courtroom, a look of utter disgust and contempt on my face. The disappointment of losing my licence was too much. I was going to be totally restricted for a whole year.

I lost a lot of things because of alcohol. It didn't do me any favours. And, despite the hardships I was forced to endure, I continued to drink. I never learned a thing from my mistakes. Alcohol dictated what to do and when and how to do it. I was a slave to the booze.

By this time my body was totally dependent on alcohol. In the silence of the night I used to wake up, shaking and sweating, my body crying out for a drink. Then I would jump out of bed, frantically searching the house for half a bottle, or even a few drops, of whisky to calm my frenzy. I had bottles hidden all over the house—under the mattress, behind the settee, in the meter-box, behind the toilet, in the wardrobe, any place I thought I could hide it without Sally finding it. After searching the gas meter I usually discovered a small bottle stashed away. Quickly I unscrewed the top and let the warm comforting liquid flood into my system. As the shaking and sweating stopped I knew that the Master had taken control again.

One summer Sally's aunt, who lived in England, came to spend a week with us. Just after she arrived I was buying myself a bottle of whisky in the local off-licence and I thought it would be a nice gesture to get Aunt Gretta a bottle of Pimms. That night I finished the entire bottle of whisky. There was no more alcohol in the house apart from the brown paper package sitting in the cupboard, the Pimms. Around four o'clock in the morning I woke abruptly out of a deep sleep, beads of sweat trickling down my forehead. I raced downstairs into the shadowy kitchen and headed straight for the Pimms. The following day, when Sally's aunt asked for a glass all that was left was an empty bottle. In desperation I had finished every last drop.

The lengths to which an alcoholic will go to get his 'fix' are incredible. I was no exception. I remember another desperate middle-of-the-night craving. Our neighbours had returned from their holiday in Spain and brought us back an ornament—a glass matador filled with Spanish brandy. As before, I woke up in the middle of the night craving a drink but could find none in the house. Then I remembered the little glass matador. I yanked off his head and drank the contents. The taste left a lot to be desired, but it satisfied my craving. When I had finished, I filled up the ornament with cold tea so that Sally wouldn't get suspicious.

But of course the effects of alcoholism are not confined to home. Looking back at that time, I am constantly surprised by the way I literally escaped with my life, over and over again. For example, one summer I spent a week with some Scottish friends in Glasgow. One of them owned a speedboat and so we decided to take it for a spin on one of the lochs. It was a beautiful day; the sky was blue with fluffy clouds, the water was calm. As usual, we had not come empty-handed and the car boot was full of alcohol. We had stopped at an off-licence and also had several stone jars of wine to liven things up a bit. Soon we were out on the loch bouncing along on the surface. I wanted to have a shot at steering the boat, so I took the wheel. We'd been drinking heavily and by this time I was pretty intoxicated. Within seconds I had run the boat aground and we all ended up shivering in the icy waters of the loch. We erupted into laughter, but in reality we could have been badly injured, or worse.

I remember vividly the night I awoke to find no drink in the house. The horror of it all is still with me. One Saturday morning, I had been out with my brother-in-law, Charlie, for a pub-crawl. We had staggered from bar to bar on the Shankill Road, totally drunk. After many hours' heavy drinking I had decided to go home for a sleep, so I took a bus up to my house. The trouble was that I had forgotten to do something. I had not made my usual trip to the off-licence for a bottle of whisky to take home. This omission proved to be a big mistake.

I went home and fell into bed. My sleep was long and deep. I didn't wake up until 4 a.m. the following morning. I jumped up, wide awake, the sheets soaked with sweat, and with beads of sweat trickling down my forehead. My whole body quaked. The intense desire for a drink had cut through my sleep, forcing me to race through the house, searching for a bottle of whisky. I looked in every nook and cranny, desperately hoping to find even a half-empty bottle. As time passed and still I'd found nothing, panic began to rise.

Eventually I found a few empty bottles and lifted them in the air to shake the contents into my mouth. A few tiny droplets of whisky hit my lips. But it wasn't enough. Now that I'd had a taste of alcohol, the craving got worse. I just had to have it. My mind was buzzing with frustration and desperation. I wanted to climb the walls; I wanted to tear the house down. Agony, despair, anguish, the realization that I couldn't cope, all these feelings ripped through my body. The shaking and sweating were uncontrollable. I couldn't bear it. I couldn't stand the loss of power over my own mind and body. A glass of whisky would give me that control. I had to have it.

I grabbed my jacket, which was draped over the top of a chair, and snatched a packet of cigarettes from the inside pocket. I thought they might calm my nerves. Some hope! I stuck a cigarette in my mouth and opened a box of matches, but my hands were shaking so badly that I could hardly light it. I smoked one cigarette after another, but it was no good. Nothing had changed.

At the point of madness, I rushed into the kitchen, filled a glass with water and tried desperately to make my mind believe that it was vodka. I concentrated, totally focusing my mind on the clear liquid in the glass.

'It's not water, it's vodka,' I told myself, and lifted the glass, trying desperately to taste vodka.

But I couldn't. I was only drinking a glass of water. I knew it and my body knew it. The craving remained unsatisfied. I was scared that I would go mad. I remember looking at my watch. It was about 6.45 a.m. I knew that the Mayo Street Club opened at half past seven. I would have to wait until then. Forty-five more minutes of hell. I paced up and down, wringing my hands in anguish. I couldn't even shave because my hands were shaking so badly. Finally I could stand it no longer, I grabbed my coat and left the house. An elderly man was walking past. I asked him the time and he told me that it was 7.30 a.m. The club would now be open.

'Would you mind if I walked down the road with you?' I asked.

He probably thought that I was some kind of nut, but he agreed anyway. Every step was an effort. I thought the ground was going to swallow me up. I wanted to run to the club, but I didn't have the energy.

As we approached Mayo Street, I started to panic. What if I was wrong about the club's opening time? I was sweating intensely.

'Oh, please God, let this club be open!' I thought. At the time I was some sort of atheist, but I was willing to cling on to absolutely anything. I was terrified and could hardly bear to look at the doors of the club in case they were closed. They were open! The room was empty. Inside, the barman was playing a one-armed bandit.

Penny after penny disappeared, as he got more engrossed in the machine. As I wandered in, he saw my face and I think that he guessed my plight. I didn't have to say anything. He just saw me shaking and knew that I needed a drink.

I asked for a glass of whisky and a bottle of Guinness. I was so weak and my hands were shaking so badly that to lift the glass of whisky to my lips took incredible effort. I had to use both hands, and finally I got the first drops into my mouth. Then I began to pour glass after glass down my throat. My whole system began to slow down. It was such a relief. I felt I could cope again. I felt in control of myself. Sleep began to overtake me, but I knew that I couldn't go home because there was no drink there. So I headed for the Loyalist Club where a friend of mine worked.

'Hello, Bobby. Listen, I've a couple of friends coming over from Scotland,' I lied. 'I've no drink in the house to give them. Could you just lend me a bottle of whisky? I'll pay you back tomorrow.'

Lying came naturally to me and Bobby was taken in by my little act. With a bottle of whisky in my hand I could go home and feel safe. I would not have to go through the utter terror of a night without a drink.

11
Attack!

As I fell apart, so did life in Belfast. I shall never forget the bombing of the Bayardo Bar in 1975. I was there. And lucky to escape with my life.

It was a Thursday night. My mate Jimmy Gillespie and I sat chatting and drinking in the lounge. The place was packed for the weekly sing-along. A young man at the front, decked out in checked shirt and jeans, strummed old country-and-western songs. All of a sudden we heard the crack of automatic gun-fire. It sounded close. Immediately the place erupted into a frenzy. My mate and I jumped up and raced towards the toilets. The attack seemed to have come from the front bar. For the moment, all was quiet. We managed to get close to the front door of the bar, but suddenly the gunmen opened fire. We turned on our heels and managed to escape. But not everyone was quite so fortunate. One of the bullets hit a young man at the door. He went down in a pool of blood, dead.

Suddenly a masked man appeared to our left and threw in a duffle-bag bomb. There was a blue flash and we hit the deck. The next things I remember are screaming, crying, darkness. The building had collapsed on top of us. I was buried under a heap of rubble, choking, gasping for air. A smell of burning hung in the air. People who a few minutes earlier had been sitting relaxing were now dead, injured, crushed, struggling for life.

I have some memory of being dug out of the rubble, free to breathe once again. Then I noticed that I wasn't wearing my jacket. It must have blown off in the explosion. I emerged from the bomb blast shocked but virtually unscathed. I was extremely concerned about my friend.

'Where's my mate?' I asked my rescuers. 'Have you found him yet? His name's Jimmy, is he OK?'

To my horror, I learned that as yet he hadn't been found.

People had come from all over the Shankill Road to help in the search for bodies. The atmosphere was electric, and desperation was clearly written on every face as people clawed through the rubble, scanning it for any trace of life. Some of the volunteers walked across a dislodged iron beam to get from one part of the building to another. What they didn't know was that this beam was lying on top of Jimmy Gillispie's chest. When this was discovered, a group of us worked together to try to remove it. After much effort and exhaustion we managed to free my friend from his agony. He was in bad shape, but still alive, much to my relief.

The bombing was a horrific experience and left many people injured and five people dead. One of them was a good friend of mine. Although I didn't know it, this experience laid the foundations for a change in my feelings towards religion. Then, I felt I couldn't believe in a God who would let evil people murder and maim so easily. But when I look back on that explosion I can see that there had to be a God and that he was looking after me. Indeed, I was involved in many situations like the Bayardo, where humanly speaking I should have been dead, but God graciously preserved my life.

Later that year I was taking some people to visit relatives in the Royal Victoria Hospital, situated on the Falls Road in the heart of Republican country. I had parked the car on the Grosvenor Road while my friends went into the hospital. The radio was playing and I was sitting staring into space when suddenly, in my rear-view mirror, I noticed two men. They came out of a bar and crossed to my side of the road. They were staring intently at my car and I began to get suspicious. They approached the vehicle, opened the back door and asked me for identity. Startled, I slipped the car into automatic drive and took off, throwing the two men on to their backs.

With my heart racing, I reached the traffic lights at the junction of the Falls Road, mounted the pavement and managed to get back to the Shankill and safety. When I stopped the car I was trembling. The realization that I had almost been captured by the Provos hit me. The two men must have been contacted by someone in the hospital when they saw the car arrive. Had they captured me I would probably have been taken over to Leeson Street or another IRA haunt and executed. Unnerved by these horrifying thoughts I headed to the local bar for a few stiff drinks.

Living with danger was a very real part of life in the 1970s. One evening I came out of the Rex Bar having had quite a bit to drink and ready to go home. I staggered across the road to wait for a black taxi and about a minute later a car came speeding up the road; a burst of gun-fire was clearly audible. Immediately I dived into an alleyway behind a bus stop. When the car had gone I picked myself up. I was a little shaken but because I'd been drinking I was not totally aware of what had happened. In fact, I began to think I had imagined the whole episode. To quell my doubts I returned to the scene the following day. Sure enough there were holes in the wall I had been standing against. Another close shave!

It was an incredibly tense period. The question uppermost in everyone's mind was 'Who is going to be next?' The threat of danger was never far from ordinary life and in a way you got used to it. You had to. One night I was standing talking to a man on the corner of the Lower Shankill Estate. It was dark and there were few people around. All of a sudden a car came flying down the Shankill Road and opened up with gun-fire. My friend and I dived behind a wall. Then it was quiet. The gun-fire stopped. We were just about to come out from our hiding-place when the car came back and opened up again. We had no idea who it was and weren't able to take the car registration number. To many people now these situations sound like cowboys and Indians, but these incidents were commonplace in areas like the Shankill. You knew that when you came out of the pubs late at night and were walking along the shadowy streets, things were likely to happen. Many men were shot dead late at night on the streets of the Shankill. But there was little you could do about the threat of attack. You either stayed at home or went for a drink and took your chances.

At that time we were constantly surrounded with death. Killings happened every day. Innocent people died as a result of being in the wrong place at the wrong time. In my permanently drunken state, I wandered into many dangerous areas. Some of the men I went out drinking with were capable of cutting my throat and it wouldn't have cost them a thought. It wasn't just the Provos I had to contend with, but my own people. You almost had to walk around Belfast with your back to the wall. You didn't know who your enemies were; you didn't know who you could talk to; you didn't know who your friends were. I realize now that it was a miracle that I came through the 70s without being killed or injured.

My love affair with booze made me vulnerable to attacks on my life. And now I praise God for his protection.

I was sitting in a bar one day when I heard shots. A group of people came running into the lounge, and I heard that one of my friends had been shot dead and another injured. The old familiar feeling of nausea rose up as I left my seat. There, in the public bar, lay Jim Semple, blood running from his mouth. My stomach lurched. He had been shot dead by a British soldier. What was worse, the bullet fired at Jim had gone straight through him and into Ray Simms. He was badly injured and in hospital for a long time afterwards.

Another friend of mine, Dave Watson, walked out of the Bayardo Bar one night to his death. He left me drunk, and said that he was going to another bar further up the Shankill Road. But he stepped straight out of the bar on to the road and was hit by at least two or three vehicles. I rushed out and a ghastly sight met my eyes. Dave's head was severed from his body. The police came and shovelled up what was left of him. All because of the poison.

12
Breakdown

By the end of the 70s my mind and body began to feel the devastating effects of alcohol abuse. For many years I had had difficulty saying certain words and now I stuttered very badly. This speech impediment added to my intense insecurity. I found it impossible to relax in a conversation, and my inferiority complex was so severe that two people talking in a pub only had to look in my direction and I felt that they were talking about me. I suppose it was a sort of persecution complex.

Booze ignited fear in my mind and almost everyone posed a threat to me—the police, the army, the IRA, UDA and UVF.* When I was drinking, as the comforting effects of alcohol began to fade, friends and foes alike alarmed me.

After hangovers I was engulfed by terrible depression. My mind was filled with thoughts of self-pity and most days I didn't want to get out of bed. To me life was a futile, empty routine.

'What's the use? What is there to get up for?' I thought to myself as I lay curled up with my whisky bottle.

The alcohol did not only assault my mind; my body was hit with a barrage of ailments. Sometimes, after a boozing session, I would be lying slumped over the settee, trying to pull myself together, when I would try to move an arm or leg and discover that I couldn't. I was momentarily paralyzed. This sudden immobility, which passed as quickly as it came, was horrific, because I didn't know if or when my movement was going to return.

My body was weak and particularly vulnerable to illness and I was continually besieged with flu, colds and stomach upsets. Every morning found me lurching over the toilet, sweat pouring out of me, vomiting violently. My aches and pains made me a familiar figure in the doctor's waiting-room. Often my doctor would write 'hypertension' on sick notes. I thought that this was something to do with my duodenal ulcer, but I soon found that it described high blood pressure, a result of my excess drinking. While others were freezing, the sweat was pouring out of my body. All these symptoms pointed to one thing—an early grave.

As if this wasn't enough, the use of valium tablets became part of my daily routine. Now I no longer felt the same surge of warmth and confidence that used to come after several hours in a pub. My system still craved the alcohol, but was so used to it that I wasn't able to get drunk as easily. That's where the valium tablets came in. When I popped the tiny white tablets into my mouth and took a swig of whisky, warmth and confidence returned. I began to see the world in a hazy light. Everything was rosy; everything was great. I didn't have to think about real life—the violence and the hatred were a million miles away. Soon I was immersed in a fantasy land and the harsh elements of life were forgotten for the time being.

I hated it when the effect wore off, though. Coming back to reality, to the dreadful life I was leading, was hell. When the drunken feelings had gone, violent shaking set in. I couldn't bear it, so I had another drink and maybe some valium. If the shaking continued, I would reach again for my little brown bottle of tablets and another glass of whisky. My system was crying out for more and the only way to pacify it was to pour in more poison. It was a vicious circle.

At this point I had some frightening sensations. On several occasions my heart started to race. I felt as if there was a time bomb inside me and it was going to explode. Once or twice Sally had to call a doctor. I thought I was dying. The doctor realized that I had been drinking and taking valium and tried to explain to me the gravity of the situation.

'Look, Mr McIlwaine. One of these days you're not going to be able to ring for a doctor. Valium tablets combined with alcohol will kill you. Your heart will stop!'

Each time I promised faithfully to quit the booze, but my promises were shortlived. I was an alcoholic and it was impossible for me to keep my vows relating to alcohol. I craved it day and night.

So once again I got up to my old tricks and once again the doctor was by my side. Several times I was whisked off to the hospital for cardiographs. But I refused to let the doctors admit me. I was in grave danger and I really needed the medical attention, but I knew that I couldn't survive in hospital without alcohol. There was no way that I could stand being confined to a bed without a drop of booze touching my lips. I would go insane. So any time that the doctors did manage to admit me I signed myself out.

One night after a very heavy drinking bout I collapsed in the Loyalist Club. The next thing that I remember is waking up and seeing screens around my bed. I smelt the familiar sterile odour and realized that I was in hospital. I felt trapped, imprisoned. I couldn't control my life, my actions. I couldn't get a drink.

'Oh, my God. I have to get out of here!' I thought.

Immediately I jumped out of bed and pulled open

my locker to search for clothes. Quickly I began to dress and then I poked my head outside the screens. The ward was quiet, there were no nurses or doctors around. At the top end a television set flickered, but most of the patients were sleeping. Seizing my chance, I gently pushed back part of the screen and walked out of the ward, trying not to look too conspicuous. There were several staff members in the sister's office but they were engrossed in conversation, so my exit went unnoticed. I found I was on the top floor of the hospital, so I thought the best way to get out would be to climb down the fire escape. After walking down a long hallway I came to a door which led outside. The hallway was empty, so quickly, my heart racing, I pushed open the door and stepped outside on to the rusty fire escape.

Fear gripped me as I saw how far I would have to climb down. I had always been afraid of heights, but I knew that this was the only way. I slowly stepped from rung to rung. Finally, much to my relief, I was back on the ground and back in the real world where I could get a drink. I walked out of the hospital gates and on to the Lisburn Road, where I hailed a taxi.

The driver told me that there were bomb scares all over Belfast and that a lot of roads would be closed. I started to panic.

'Look, I'll pay you whatever you want, if you can just get me home!'

It was early in the morning and no pubs would be open, but I knew that I had a bottle of whisky stashed in the meter-box at home. The taxi driver, eager for a few extra pounds, agreed to get me home and somehow he did. After paying him, I raced straight into the front room where the meter-box was. I threw open the door and grabbed the large bottle of whisky which was hidden inside. I was standing drinking when the phone rang. My wife walked into the room to answer the phone and was shocked when she saw me. She lifted the phone to be told by a doctor that I had escaped.

'Yes I know,' she said. 'He's standing here drinking a bottle of whisky.'

The doctor wanted to speak to me, but I refused. I knew that he would try to persuade me to return to the hospital. There was no way that I was giving in. The only reason that I had been in the hospital was that I had collapsed; I didn't go of my own accord. Looking back, I'm sure the medical staff were fed up with me because I was constantly being admitted to hospital and then signing myself out. It was then that the doctors told me that, if I didn't quit the drink, I would be dead in a couple of years. Most of their words went unheeded.

Nevertheless, there were two occasions in 1977 and 1978 when I was so ill that I was forced to stay in the hospital. In 1977 I had returned home from the pub and began throwing up clots of blood. Sally immediately called an ambulance and I was rushed into the City Hospital with internal bleeding. X-rays showed that excessive drinking had enlarged my liver. One of the doctors, a small oriental man, explained the situation.

'Look Mr McIlwaine,' he said gravely, 'if you don't stop drinking, you will develop cirrhosis of the liver in a very short space of time.' He continued, 'We would like you to be admitted to the Shaftesbury Square Alcoholic Hospital to be dried out.'

'No way, doctor!' I bellowed. 'I'm not going in there with all those down-and-outs and skid row people. All they drink is Brasso and methylated spirits. I drink nothing but the best. I'm not an alcoholic!'

In fact I promised the doctors that I would kick the booze and I did try to keep my promise. I felt that if I had some sort of hobby or pastime it would fill the space that the booze occupied. So I bought myself a set of fishing rods and set off to a nearby river to see what I could catch. All I ended up catching was a cold! My fishing fad didn't last very long. So I headed back to the one thing that I could trust to fill the huge vacuum that existed in my life.

In 1978 I was back in hospital once again. The doctor who had treated me the previous year refused to deal with me.

'If you want to commit suicide, go ahead! But you're not going to waste my time!' he told me.

After several blood transfusions the doctors managed to stop the bleeding. I was told that my once enlarged liver was now shrinking and hardening. I was developing cirrhosis of the liver. Again the doctors asked me to consider drying out at the alcoholics' hospital, but still I refused. However, I knew that somehow I would have to quit drinking or I would end up dead. I thought mind over matter was the answer. For five long weeks I managed to conquer my obsession and control my mind. But one day it snapped.

It was the Tuesday after Easter. The junior Orangemen were parading down the Shankill Road and I stood watching. Suddenly the flute bands launched into a rendition of 'The Sash'. On hearing this old Loyalist song, I began to feel emotional. A few friends of mine were standing across the road at the Rex Bar.

'I have to have a drink!' I thought, beads of sweat breaking on my forehead. 'Just one won't do any harm.'

I told the people I was standing with that I was going for a drink.

'Don't go back to it, Billy,' one man said. 'You're gonna kill yourself!'

'Look, I just don't care any more,' I replied. 'I just

83

can't stay away. I'd rather be dead than go through life like this.'

I crossed the road and entered the alluring doors of the Rex Bar. After having a beer, I made an excuse to go to another bar, supposedly to buy cigarettes. I planted myself on a bar stool and staggered out a few hours and many glasses of whisky later. I was back on the booze again, this time for good.

* UDA = Ulster Defence Association, UVF = Ulster Volunteer Force

13
Death's Door

The long icy winter of 1979 turned to spring. All around me nature was bursting into new life, but my life was ebbing away. I realized that my time on earth was coming to an end. To kick the booze was an impossible feat, so I resigned myself to an early grave.

Although I was only thirty-six, physically I was like an old man. My health was deteriorating rapidly and I no longer had the strength to go to the pubs or the off-licence. There was no light at the end of this tunnel.

Most of my days were spent sprawled across the settee with my constant companion—a bottle of whisky—at my side. Usually I tried to have a good stock of alcohol hidden around the house, but one night the supply dried up. I had drained every bottle for the last drop but this did not satisfy the furious hunger inside. I shook the bottles violently, but they refused to yield any more. They were totally empty. I knew that this meant I would have to make the long and physically draining trek to the off-licence down the road. By this stage I couldn't go alone. I thought that if I could take my daughter Rhonda down with me, she could help me walk. I realized that Sally would probably refuse to let her go, but it was worth a try. So I posed the question to her. She turned to me with a horrified look on her face.

'You must be out of your mind!' Sally snapped. 'There's no way you're taking that child with you to buy your booze! Don't you think she's been through enough?'

Panic bells began to ring inside me. I was shaking and sweating profusely; I buried my head in my hands. Sally looked at me and somehow she must have seen it was a genuine cry for help. She realized how desperately I needed a drink and put her hand on my shoulder.

'I'll go with you,' she quietly said.

We walked together in the cool night air down the Ballygomartin Road towards the off-licence, where I bought a large bottle of whisky. As we walked home, intense pains shot down my side and I held on to Sally tightly. I had had no food for several days, my body was weak and limp and a powerful feeling of nausea churned in my stomach. But I never told my wife just how ill I was. Afterwards I found out that all this time she thought I was hell-bent on destroying myself. She had no idea that by now I had no choice. I suppose I had never said that I couldn't control my drinking. Indeed, I'd never looked at the situation rationally and decided that I would carry on boozing. There had been no decision. Now I just couldn't stop. Sally, like most people, did not understand alcoholism or the compulsion within the alcoholic which drives him on until humanly speaking there is no way out.

Those times when I was able to venture out of the house, I headed for the nearby Mountainview Social Club on the Woodvale Road. I became friendly with a few of the men there and we used to sit drinking and playing cards together. The off-licence was just around the corner and I used to leave the club early so that I could get there before closing time. Once I had a bottle of whisky in my hand I was safe and secure. To go home without that alcohol would be a total nightmare; it had happened before and I knew that I could never endure such hell again. Right now I was at a point in my life where either consuming alcohol or being forced to go through withdrawal could kill me.

Thoughts of old friends such as Glenn Barnes and Raymond Jones used to swim though my head. Both had died from cirrhosis of the liver. I'd watched both men as they had progressed along the downward slope of alcoholism. Traits I had seen in them were now a part of me. I was getting weaker and weaker. When I walked I staggered. My balance was bad, I just couldn't walk straight and I seemed to be walking on my heels rather than the balls of my feet. And this happened when I wasn't even drunk. Alcohol had destroyed my co-ordination.

Night after night I lay in bed, my eyes fixed on the shadowy walls, my hands gripping my sides as the pain jabbed constantly. I hardly ever had a full night's sleep, there was no escape from my horrific life. I had given up on going to doctors. I was sick of hearing their lectures on how I was abusing my body with alcohol. Death was imminent and I began to accept its approach.

For many years the Orange Order had been the pride of my life. The Whiterock Parade was held on the last Saturday in June and launched the summer's marching season. Although I was on my last legs, I was still determined to walk in this parade. I psyched myself up and made myself believe that somehow my body would be capable of doing it.

'If I can only do this,' I thought, 'it will change everything. My condition will improve.'

The morning of the parade dawned. I knew that this day would make or break me. I had very little to drink, maybe just a few glasses of beer, but not enough to intoxicate me. I got ready, put on some decent clothes and placed the orange collarette around my neck.

'I don't look too bad,' I thought as I studied my reflection in the mirror.

The suit and orange collarette seemed to smarten up my appearance. But then I was only fooling myself, because it didn't change the person underneath. I was still feeling the same.

Around 1 p.m. the parade set off, snaking its way up the Shankill Road and down the narrow side streets. Wanting to look big, it was not enough for me just to walk in the parade; I offered to carry the banner. Looking back, it seems ridiculous that I even took part. I was a dying man and I could hardly walk straight, never mind support a large banner. Many of the onlookers who knew me saw me stagger all over the road and thought I was drunk.

'Look at him,' I heard an old woman mutter. 'He's a disgrace to the Orange Order!'

As the march went on, every step seemed to drain me of energy. Then my vision began to get misty, and then there were three of everything in front of my eyes. Finally I could go no further, my whole body failing and a mass of disease. I collapsed and the banner went down with me. Thinking that these were the antics of a drunken man, some of the men in the lodge came and picked up the banner, leaving me lying at the side of the road. The parade passed by and I was left like a discarded piece of rubbish.

I lay with my face in the dirt, my hands gripping my sides, as if trying to protect myself from the acute pains that stabbed me so violently. My strength was gone and I lay paralyzed with pain. My pride lay in the gutter with me. All my life the Orange Order had been my passion, my pride, my joy. Now I was nothing but a humiliation, I was a disgrace. Everyone had thought that I was drunk, as my face was so bloated and my co-ordination so bad. In reality I was on the way out.

This incident totally destroyed my ego. I had publicly shamed myself in front of the organization I loved. My Orange brethren had abandoned me, I was nothing but a let-down. I had lost every shred of respect that I may have had in the Orange Order and in the community as a whole. So what else was there to live for? Life was something to be endured; the world was empty and hostile. Everything was falling apart at the seams; the end was coming. I lost heart. I lost the will to live. That was June. But what about July?

July is a particularly festive month for Northern Ireland's Protestant community. The 11th and 12th are the most important dates in the Loyalist calendar. Since I was a boy I had always loved the merriment of the eleventh night. For many months local kids sweated, building up huge bonfires from wood, old furniture and any other scraps people cared to give them. All their hard work was rewarded when the fires were set alight late on the eleventh night. There was always a buzz, a real tingling in the air, as I strolled around the different fires. Afterwards everyone went to the pubs and clubs for a boozing session. Perhaps one of the Scottish bands (who travelled over every year for the festivities) would have brought their flutes and drums and the place would rock with the singing of Loyalist party songs. Finally at three or four in the morning I would stagger home, fall into bed for a few hours and then take part in the huge Orange parade the next day. Ever since I had joined the Orange Order I had never missed participating in the Twelfth parade. I couldn't imagine life without it.

It was the highlight of a year—the day we demonstrated our opposition to the Catholics and our pride in King William and the Protestant cause. Thousands of people lined the route and clapped the bands and Orangemen as they walked by.

But for me 1979 was different. I could barely move off the settee, never mind walk around bonfires or go on a march. I had always thought of it as a great honour to take part in such a demonstration of strength. But this year I was housebound. The only way that I would see the parade would be on a television screen.

Two days later the cirrhosis of the liver had moved into its final stage. Stormy seas of confusion raged in my mind. *Where am I? Who am I?* Questions sprang at me like fiery darts. I couldn't find the answers. Suddenly fragments, glimpses of light, flooded into my dark, inner tunnel and I began to recall the events of the previous day.

Early in the morning my wife and daughter had left for a holiday in southern Ireland. A family holiday had been the plan. Sally had thought I was drunk and I didn't bother to enlighten her. Our relationship was at an all-time low, so she had left me in my 'drunken stupor', as she supposed.

I lay alone with my pain and my thoughts. I wasn't drunk and couldn't get drunk. Long hours of perpetual drinking stretched ahead of me, drinking which didn't intoxicate me or fill that craving for warmth and security. My whole system was beginning to reject the booze and its poisoning effects and every gulp from the whisky bottle led to vomiting. Lack of food made me weak and faint, and my head was pounding. I stretched out on the floor, arching my spine in a bid to ease the sharp pains which shot from the back to the front of my body, stabbing at my lower abdomen. But it was no use, my body was deteriorating fast, surrendering to the poison which had been eating away at it for over twenty years.

Perhaps more severe than the physical pain,

however, was the mental agony. Locked in my home, the thought of dea.ℎ possessed me. I realized that my life was ebbing away and I was edging towards that dark deep valley from which there is no return. My heart was beating irregularly and I knew that each breath could be my last. The warm, numb, drunken feeling did not come, neither did feelings of victory or glory, only a crazy frenzied panic.

These mental and physical torments continued for many hours. Finally I attempted to stagger into the kitchen, but a frightening burning sensation flared up in my neck, and I found myself in a heap on the floor, momentarily paralyzed. I knew the end had come unless... unless, I could reach the phone and dial for an ambulance. Suddenly, the hospital symbolized a haven of hope. A burst of sheer will-power rose up in me and I gathered all my resources to crawl to the phone and utter a garbled message.

Within five minutes I could hear the sound of a siren and, using the last reserves of my energy, I reached up to open the door for the ambulance man. After that the memories are misty, until I arrived at the hospital reception.

In the distance I heard a faint voice, 'I don't seem to be able to get his blood pressure, it's so low, and his heart beat is irregular,' it said.

Fear shot through me. I had somehow expected an immediate magic formula from the hospital, not this doom and gloom. My next memories are the powerful jabs of a syringe and then ten days of horrific, satanic hallucinations, which stretched my mind and sanity to their limits...

Huge television screens flickered all over the walls and the ward swam with a myriad of colours, sounds and images. I watched this bizarre scene astounded. Later, as I lay in my bed staring up at the ceiling, it collapsed suddenly on top of the ward. Bricks and plaster were flying everywhere and in the horror of the event I began to shout. I was unhurt, but all around me the ward was covered in debris. Using some choice language I began to yell at the medical staff.

'Look at the mess this ward is in!' I bellowed to the bemused nurses. 'It's a disgrace. You'd better get it cleaned up!'

The following day I was just about to drift off to sleep when all of a sudden huge black bats began to ooze out of the walls. One after another these sinister-looking creatures squeezed out of the plaster and then swiftly flew towards my bed, their beady red eyes burning into me. Then, before I could protect myself, their massive wings were in my face, beating against me, stabbing me furiously. Stinging pain pierced my head and I lifted my hands to try to protect myself. But it was no good. The threatening black mass began to engulf me. Then, as quickly as it had begun, the ordeal was over. The dark fiends were gone.

None of these experiences were dreams, but they were not real either. These were the mental agony of the DTs (*delirium tremens*)—the horrifying delusions which come with alcohol withdrawal. These terrifying hallucinations came from nowhere and I had no control over the bizarre images my mind created.

For much of my stay in hospital, I was confined to a cot. I had previously made several attempts to climb out of bed, but because my balance was affected I had usually ended up in a heap on the floor. The restraining bars on my bed were to keep me in one place. Now I felt trapped, chained up like some wild animal. I was not able to eat solid food, so I was fed intravenously, hooked up to a large drip. But at times I began to rip the needles out of my arms, not caring about the danger this put me in.

When she heard about it all Sally rushed home from holiday. I remember her first visit. Her face was pale with grief and there were dark shadows under her eyes. For many years she had expected the alcohol to take its toll, but now it was actually happening. Later two other friends of mine came up to the hospital with Sally. Dorothy had worked as a secretary for me for a few years and, as she stood and looked into my swollen yellow face, she began to cry. She told me later that death seemed to be hovering over me, there didn't seem to be any hope.

One afternoon as I lay curled up in bed, bright sunlight streamed in through the window and my mind drifted in and out of reality. Then I saw two vaguely familiar figures coming towards me. Staring at them for a moment, I was able to recall who they were. I had known James Forsyth and Alastair McComish since my boyhood. Both were pastors in the Church of God on the Shankill Road, the church I had once attended and where Sally was now a member.

The two men did the customary reading and praying that ministers do when they visit the sick, and it didn't mean a thing to me. I felt that their prayers were going no higher than the ceiling. God was only an illusion, only a crutch that people had dreamt up to enable them to cope with life. There was no divine force controlling this world. If there was, then why was he allowing me to go through this hell on earth? I appreciated James and Alastair's visit, but I had no time for their God.

A few days later James came to see me again. He asked me how I was feeling, but I didn't answer him. Something in the corner was attracting my attention.

'What are you staring at, Billy?' James asked me.

'Do you see that big oil tanker over there in the corner? It's been there for the past week being re-fuelled,' I replied.

James looked at me, puzzled.

'I don't see any oil tanker,' he said.

'Ah, but you're looking at the wrong wall!'

It's funny now, but it shows the complete absurdity of someone suffering from the DTs. During those days nothing seemed to be real. I used to look at the nurses and see the faces of my nieces. This made me wonder why so many of my family were working in the hospital. The doctors constantly questioned me, trying to find out if I had any grasp on reality.

'Do you have any idea where you are, Mr McIlwaine?' they asked.

'What a stupid question. I'm in a hotel of course!' I answered abruptly.

Sally was constantly forced to listen to my wild and crazy ramblings. I used to tell her that I had been given a shovel and put to work digging, down in the yard. My mind had completely gone.

Facing my bed lay an old priest, a Monsignor in the Catholic church. He was dying. One night while I was lying looking over at the old priest's bed, three men came in carrying crates of booze. After seating themselves around the bed, they began to tuck into the bottles of alcohol. About ten minutes later two of the men left and returned with a large wooden coffin into which they placed the dying priest.

I remember thinking, 'They're putting that old man in a coffin and he's not even dead.'

Then they started to stuff his nose with cotton wool. By this time I was shouting. When they grabbed the coffin and ran out I yelled, 'They're stealing that man's body!'

I thought that I had seen the last of them, but suddenly they reappeared with the coffin, put it on the bed and continued to drink.

'My God!' I thought. 'You can't get away from

drink anywhere. They're even carrying it into the hospitals!'

This incident of course was a hallucination, but as far as I was concerned, it had actually happened. The next day when Sally arrived, I started to unfold the tale.

'There were men in here last night,' I said in an excited tone, 'and they carried out that old man's body in a coffin!'

At that point I noticed that the priest's bed was shrouded by screens and this horrified me. Again I started ranting and raving and, in order to calm me, Sally asked the nurses to pull back the screens so that I could see that the old man was all right. The screens were removed and there was the old man. He was very ill, but still alive. Even seeing the man for myself did not erase the horror of the previous night from my mind.

I spent a lot of time gazing over at the old priest. I watched his shrivelled frail body as he struggled for every breath. At any moment I expected to hear that desperate gasping for air cease and then nothing—just silence. This terrified me because I knew that this was my fate too.

One afternoon my sister May came to visit me, carrying a bunch of the most vibrant red roses.

'Look what I've brought, Billy,' she said, presenting me with the blooms. 'Aren't they beautiful?'

I was horrified. Those petals were bleeding. Huge drops of thick blood were pouring on to the floor forming a crimson pool. During my sister's visit I tried to conceal my terror, but once she had gone I called one of the nurses over and asked her to remove them.

'I'm sorry, Mr McIlwaine. I can't do that,' she said. 'Your sister brought the flowers for you.'

'Look, please do what I ask! I can't stand those awful things near me!' I shouted.

'All right, all right, calm down. Don't be getting yourself into a state,' she said, lifting the roses.

After arranging them in a vase, the nurse placed them on the old priest's locker. A short time later the desperate breathing on the other side of the room stopped. The priest was dead.

'Thank God I got rid of those flowers,' I thought, 'or it would have been me.' The DTs had warped my mind.

A few days later, as I lay staring out the window one morning, I saw what appeared to be a cross. A tall figure clad in a white robe stood on a hill behind it. I recognized the figure as Jesus. Suddenly out of the corner of my eye I noticed huge scarlet creatures racing up and down the ward. We had been invaded by giant crabs. These evil, menacing-looking creatures began to come towards me and I was stricken with fear. I couldn't move, I was too weak to run away. I looked out of the window and Jesus was looking at me sympathetically. He walked down the hill and into the ward. At his presence the crabs began to flee. He simply waved them aside with his hands and they disappeared into the walls. Then he stood beside my bed, a look of compassion shining from his face, his faint smile reassuring me that everything would be all right. After a moment, he left my bed and returned to the cross on the hill.

Only those who have been through the horror of the DTs can fully grasp what I've described. So many times I seemed to be descending into the eternal gloom of the valley of death, but something or someone suddenly hauled me out of the shadows and back into reality. Looking back I can see that even in the midst of these horrific hallucinations God was with me, he was caring for me. Even then, I had to travel through hell and back. I learned my lesson the hard way.

14

Metamorphosis

Ten days had crawled by, or was it ten minutes, or ten years? I had no concept of time. Sleep would not come. The darkness cast shadows which threatened to engulf me. They played tricks on my eyes. Then, in the stillness, images began to dance before me. I saw myself, the life I had lived, flash in front of me. Was that really me? Had I really treated my family that way? The selfish man I had become didn't care about anyone but himself—didn't care about his wife or daughter or anyone else.

It was like watching a fast-forwarding video tape. Countless pictures raced by, each one a reflection of the self-centred human being I had become. Suddenly the images faded into the shadows, leaving me stunned with the awful reality of my life. Left alone in the blackness, I knew that change had to come, but I couldn't transform myself. The time had come to yield to the God who for so many years I had denied.

I knew that it was time for me to turn to God. The sins of my past weighed heavily on my shoulders, crushing me. I desperately needed release. I cried out to God, 'Do you think that you could find it in your heart to forgive a man like me for all the things that I've done?'

Tears of remorse rolled down my face and at that moment I desired God's love and mercy more than life itself. And God saw those tears, he saw sincere repentance and he answered my urgent cry for help.

'If you're truly sorry, if you really repent of the things that you have done, you will be forgiven,' he said.

That night as I lay confined to my hospital bed I experienced intensely the enveloping presence of God. I was no longer alone; I had a friend whom the Bible says sticks closer than a brother. He wasn't some intangible, unreachable spirit looking down from heaven; he was in my heart, flooding my whole being with his wonderful love. I continued to talk to him.

'Lord, I'm sorry for all the terrible things I've done in my life. Cleanse me of all the sin that I've committed. Change my life and make me a new man.'

At that moment I experienced the most tremendous release. The weight which pinioned and trapped me was suddenly removed and I was free to breathe once again. Although my body was harnessed to many drips and tubes, my spirit soared. I felt as though shackles had been unclasped from my feet, that I had been led out of the depths of a dungeon into the bright sunlight of day. All fear, all anxiety was driven out. I had handed what was left of my life to the God who made me. A profound peace flooded through me and I knew at this point that I was ready to meet him. And I told him that if he would let me live, I would make a solemn promise.

'I will serve you all the days of my life,' I vowed to God, 'and I'll take the gospel to Catholics and Protestants all over Ireland. I will preach your love and forgiveness to the whole community.'

God spoke into my heart.

'You will live,' he told me. 'You will again enjoy health and strength. You're not going to die, you're going to serve me and work for me.'

At this moment my hope was renewed. For me there

was no question of how a body so poisoned with alcohol and close to death could be restored to health. I clung to that marvellous promise—I was going to live!

About half an hour later, I was lying simply communing with God, when out of the corner of my eye I saw a familiar face staring down at me. My friend John Chambers had popped in for a quick visit. I was surprised to see him, but I was desperate to tell someone of my incredible experience.

'John, I've got some great news for you,' I began.

I was so enthusiastic, so full of zeal that I could hardly get the words out quickly enough.

'About half an hour ago I accepted the Lord into my heart. I'm a Christian.'

A look of utter disbelief was clearly written on my friend's face. In the past week I had said so many crazy things while in the midst of the DTs that John simply felt that this was another of my ridiculous remarks.

'Do you really understand what you're saying to me?' he asked.

'Yes I do,' I answered. 'I've had enough of the booze. I'm finished with my old way of life, only God can sort me out now.'

John was astounded both by my words and the clarity with which I was speaking. Now he could see that these were not the wild ramblings of some madman, but the words of a person who had had a very real spiritual experience, a person who had met Christ.

That night when John left the hospital he raced straight up to my house to tell Sally. My wife had stuck by me through ten years of hellish drinking and despite it all she loved me. I didn't know it, but Sally had prayed for me continually, asking God to save me. In one night God had answered a decade of prayer and Sally was to see the fruits of her labour.

However, like John, she was sceptical of my conversion.

'Are you sure he's not hallucinating?' she asked him.

But John was positive that I was in my right mind.

'I really believe that he knows what he's saying, Sally. Anyway, you'll see when you go to visit him tomorrow.'

That night I fell into an amazingly still and peaceful slumber. During my stay in hospital I had suffered from intense insomnia. My mind had been infused with thoughts of death and the utter terror of leaving this life had allowed no rest. Even when I had managed to fall into some kind of doze, I had been haunted by demonic dreams, waking up shaking and sweating. But that July night I drifted into a beautiful sleep. God had given me peace with myself and with him.

After breakfast the following morning, the consultant approached my bed with a string of junior doctors behind him. They stood around my bed, staring at me intently as if I were some kind of specimen.

'How are you feeling this morning, Mr McIlwaine?' the consultant asked.

'Actually, doctor, I'm feeling very good,' I replied.

He looked at me strangely, probably wondering how a dying man could give such an answer. But, despite his disbelief, I went on to tell him of my experience the night before.

'The Lord appeared at my bedside last night, doctor. I asked him to forgive all my sins and he did. He healed my body and told me that I was going to live.'

The consultant turned to the junior doctors and motioned to them as if I was going mad. They had heard my ranting and raving during the DTs, and now I was rambling about God visiting me. This man really thought I had cracked up. He moved away from my bed and pacified me by saying, 'That's fine, Mr McIl-waine.'

I knew in my heart that he didn't believe me.

I really wanted to share my story with someone who would not greet it with scepticism. I needed an understanding ear. I was in a Catholic hospital where quite a few of the nurses were nuns, and later that morning I saw one of the sisters walking down the ward. Because of my upbringing, if there was one thing I had always hated in the Catholic Church it was nuns. I thought they brought bad luck and I used to spit on the ground every time I saw one. However, on this particular morning, I had no hesitation in calling the nun over to my bedside. Despite the fact that a huge crucifix hung round her neck, I asked her, 'Sister, do you believe in God?'

I really did not know what Catholics believed. The nun looked at me, smiling.

'Yes, I do,' she said.

'Would you believe me if I said that God was here last night and that he's forgiven all my sins?'

She replied that she would.

'God healed my body, sister, and he told me that he's going to give me back my health and strength,' I continued. 'What do you think of that?'

'I believe it is very possible,' she said.

At last someone was accepting my words as truth instead of fantasy. Perhaps I got overexcited, because I went on to say, 'Could you arrange to get me out of this hospital, sister?'

At this the nun backed off a little. 'You're a very sick man, Mr McIlwaine. We just can't do things like that.'

She walked away and told one of the doctors what I had said. He got a totally wrong impression and thought that I was going to sign myself out immediately, so he rushed over to my bed, extremely concerned.

'You're very ill, Mr McIlwaine!' he said in an authoritative tone. 'There are so many clubs and pubs and shibeens in Belfast that if you left this hospital you'd fall into the first one you came across.'

I told him that this would not happen. 'I'm not going back to my old way of life,' I said with determination. 'I'm finished with alcohol.'

'That's all very well, Mr McIlwaine. But all your old drinking pals will be there waiting for you when you get out.'

'Well,' I replied, 'they may be waiting for me but I'm not going back to them. I'll be making new friends, people who go to church and not pubs.'

The doctor was concerned about my poor state of health. 'The chances of you coming through this, with so much damage to your liver and pancreas, are very slim,' he said. 'Forget about going home, rest and try to eat.'

Much to the doctor's surprise, I nodded my head in agreement. Although I was anxious to get out of hospital, right now I knew I wasn't going anywhere.

That afternoon Sally arrived. She pulled up a chair and sat down at the side of my bed. Her hands were clasped together and she looked nervous, as if she was about to ask me some all-important question.

'Have you anything to tell me, Billy?' she began.

'Well, last night I accepted the Lord. I'm a Christian,' I said in a matter-of-fact way.

I told her about my conversion as if it were just something very normal and everyday—instead of a total metamorphosis in the life of an atheistic, alcoholic, violent man.

Sally was overjoyed, her eyes filled with tears and she threw her arms around me and held me tightly. It was an emotional moment. All her years of waiting, hoping, praying, were over. Here in front of her, in the weak, diseased body of her husband, was faith rewarded. God had honoured her for her patience and perseverance. For years our lives had been separate, but now we were united in Jesus Christ.

That day when I became a Christian was the turning-point. But all my problems didn't suddenly resolve themselves. Indeed, Jesus never promised that we would sail through a carefree existence, but what he did promise was that he would be with us through every storm and every battle in life.

In the next few weeks I began to see very clearly what the battle was. For almost twenty years, God's enemy, Satan, had had me firmly in his grip and he was not prepared to release me from the darkness too easily. As a new Christian my faith was fragile. I had just come through the mental agony of DTs, my mind was weak and open to attack. So Satan used the strategy of sowing doubt and fear in my mind about the experience I had had.

'The thing which you thought happened to you was all in your imagination. You're not really a Christian, you've committed too much sin in your life for God to forgive you,' whispered a voice in my ear.

'You're not going to live. You will die!' the enemy insisted.

In the stillness of the night, the mental battle intensified. No longer were there doctors and nurses hustling and bustling about. A terrible quiet descended over the whole ward, and that's when Satan moved in to torment my mind. I was haunted by thoughts of death. Almost everyone in the ward was very seriously ill, although I was right next to the sister's office under her watchful eye, so it's safe to say I was the worst.

One particular night the spirit of death seemed to be hovering over that ward. The man in the next bed got up to go to the bathroom and the next moment he was in a heap on the floor, gasping for life. He had gone into cardiac arrest. Immediately there were nurses and doctors on the scene trying desperately to get him to fight for his life. They tried to resuscitate him; his body jolted, but there was nothing there. It seemed as if all the life had been sucked out of him.

'One more time. Let's try one more time,' I heard a doctor say behind the screens. 'Stand clear!'

Then I heard the heart monitor go dead...

'There's no heartbeat doctor. He's gone,' a nurse said.

Just minutes before this man had been alive; now he had passed out of this life. Spasms of fear shot through me, but still I clung to the promise that God had given me: I was healed and I would live. I was going to work for him.

There is a verse in the Bible which says, 'Behold, old things have passed away, all things become new.' As a new Christian this verse became very real to me. In fact, I literally experienced newness of life, not only in my spirit but in my body also. Just after that momentous night, all my skin peeled off. The skin on my feet actually came off like plimsolls and underneath I had brand new skin. The medical staff were astounded; they had never seen anything like it. I just thought that it was all part of being a 'new creation'. Now, when I look back, I can see that it was a really miraculous event, in that God renewed me not only on the inside but on the outside also.

Sally bought me a beautiful black Bible and also a book called *The Power of Positive Thinking* by Dr Norman Vincent Peale. In recent years this book has come under a lot of criticism from evangelical Christians for a number of reasons. But I would say that I owe Dr Peale a lot. His book really spoke to my heart. At that time I desperately needed confidence, something to hold on to to give me strength. I read the Bible but at that point I didn't understand a lot. Peale's book was filled with many simple but profound truths. They just seemed to spring at me. Each one seemed to apply to me.

One Bible verse which Peale emphasizes is found in Paul's letter to the Philippians, chapter four and verse thirteen: 'I can do all things through Christ who strengthens me.' The book advised speaking that verse over and over again. So I did. When things seemed to be going wrong in the ward and the spirit of death seemed to be hovering, I started to quote those words. In the Bible, God's 'word' is described as being 'sharper than a two-edged sword'. So, armed with the word of God, I was able to cut through the devil's web of deception. In this way God seemed to infuse me with strength and confidence. Each time the enemy whispered another lie into my ear, I answered with the word of God.

The day dawned when I was to be discharged from hospital. I had been getting stronger and stronger and the doctors had seen the improvement. After a few weeks of intravenous feeding, I was now able to eat a little solid food. I was also able to stroll up and down the ward. How different I was from the dying man who had been rushed in a few weeks before—a raving, ranting lunatic whose life was ebbing away. Then God had reached down and turned my life around. Now a man who had been given only a few weeks to live was about to leave the hospital to begin a new life.

On the morning when I left ward five of the Mater Hospital, I was still weak and shaky. But I knew that God would continue to strengthen me. He had lifted me out of the valley of death and had promised me complete healing. Feelings and symptoms were no longer the absolute guide to my state of health. If I believed that my body would be renewed, then God would renew it.

Sally brought me some clothes for leaving hospital. She had had to buy trousers and borrow a jacket, because most of my decent clothes had ended up in the pawn shop window to supply me with money for booze. I dressed quickly, pulled back the screens and said hurried goodbyes to the medical staff who had cared for me so well. Then I walked out of ward five and into the biggest battle of my life.

15

The Battles Begin

The decision to renounce alcohol was only one battle in a long and furious war. For many years I had faced the world with a glass in my hand; now the old source of my confidence was gone. God was my new master: I had to depend on him totally.

As I passed through the iron gates of the Mater Hospital, gone were safety and security. I was confronting the cold light of day.

I returned home. My surroundings were familiar, but I was seeing them through new eyes. I was different. A new man came to live in 75 Ballygomartin Road. The drunk who had been taken away a few weeks before was never to return.

But the battle to maintain my new lifestyle was a painful one. To experience withdrawal from alcohol is to experience hell on earth. Shaking and profuse sweating were the norm for those initial 'dry' months. I had been told by the doctors that withdrawal could kill me.

I knew the road to liberation from the booze would be hard, but little did I realize how hard, or how long it would take. I experienced withdrawal symptoms for a long time. The weeks of constant battling with the old me turned into months. Many a morning I woke up paralyzed with fear of the struggles that a new day would bring. Not only was I warring with my own flesh but against the Prince of Darkness—Satan. For twenty years he had controlled my life and he wasn't going to relinquish his stronghold that easily.

The mind is probably the most sensitive and vulnerable part of the body and this is where Satan launched his vicious attack. He constantly shot arrows of fear into my thought-life—fear of insanity, and fear of death. The enemy employed every possible weapon to destroy my mind. All I had to counter his evil was a simple Bible verse: 'I can do all things through Christ who strengthens me.'

Powerful in its simplicity, this verse was my chief weapon against Satan. I lived these words and it was their strength which sustained me through those dark months.

Some days I would simply be sitting in the living room when suddenly I would find myself gripped by fear. Then I would start crying for no reason. The remedy was to race to the phone and call the nursery where Sally worked. Within minutes she would be home comforting me, encouraging me and, most importantly, praying for me. Still Satan hammered away at my mind. When someone has been in deep darkness and then comes into the light of God I believe that Satan sends every demon from hell against them to try to win them back. This was my experience.

Even though I believed that I was healed, I still experienced sharp spasms of pain. This is where faith comes in—faith does not rest on feelings. I knew that God had spoken to me in the hospital. I knew I was saved and healed. I hung on to a verse from Paul's letter to the Romans: 'If you confess with your mouth, "Jesus is Lord," and believe in your heart that God raised him from the dead, you will be saved.'

Many times when I was lying on the settee, perhaps meditating or reading, suddenly it felt as if there were a knife ripping through my stomach, pulling me in two. The agony of this sensation surged through my whole being; the torment was incredible. But despite this I held on to God. I clung to the Lord as I had once clung to alcohol. I couldn't get enough of reading the Bible or talking to him. My relationship with God was my lifeline and I knew that he would give me ultimate victory over the powers of darkness that sought to destroy me. I reminded myself of a verse in the first chapter of the book of Joshua—that if we meditate on God's word 'day and night' then we will be 'prosperous and successful'. That's what was happening to me. I was beginning to have some success against the enemy.

I would say to anyone in a struggle against alcohol: get before God in prayer; seek him morning, noon and night. I spent hour after hour on my knees crying out to him. 'Lord, don't let the devil take me back,' I pleaded. 'Keep me in the palm of your hand.'

In the early weeks of my withdrawal from the booze I was only able to eat a little physical food, but spiritual food I was able to digest quite easily. It was that which kept me alive. When panic attacks struck, when I felt like climbing the walls, I would reach for that life-sustainer, the Bible. As I was reminded of all the promises of God, renewed strength would flood through my being. I treasured those times alone with the Lord and guarded them fiercely. In fact, when my pastor or people from the church came to visit me I actually got a little annoyed because it was robbing me of my time alone with the Lord. At that point I was enjoying his fellowship so much that really I didn't need many other people.

But people like Alistair McComish, a pastor from the local church, were a real encouragement to me. Alistair had been a friend of mine since our boyhood and I felt able to confide in him the horror of what I was going through. In turn he was able to encourage me to persevere and trust God. One morning I had just had some breakfast and was reading the Bible when there was a knock at the door. It was Alistair.

'You look tired, Billy,' he said. 'Didn't you sleep last night?'

'I never sleep well,' I replied, yawning. 'Satan always seems to attack my mind in the darkness. He starts dropping thoughts of fear and death so that I don't get any rest.'

Alistair gave me some advice then that I've never forgotten.

'When that happens, just say the name "Jesus" and keep repeating it until you find yourself going off to sleep.'

That night, as I lay in the blackness, Satan started to shoot his evil thoughts into my mind. As soon as I started whispering the name of Jesus, as Alistair had recommended, they left. There's power, peace and love in the name of Jesus and I would recommend anyone experiencing satanic attack to say that name over and over and the devil will leave you.

As the weeks passed some sense of normality came back into my life. I was able to eat solid food, but only in small quantities because alcohol abuse had shrunk my stomach. My physical health and my mental state continued to improve and my appearance began to reflect this.

Alcohol had turned me into an old man who cared little about how he looked. For a long time, my black greasy hair had not seen a pair of scissors, my red face had been swollen up like a huge tomato and my eyes had been a jaundiced yellow. My weight had ballooned. Once a slim young man, I had sported a huge beer-belly. By the time I was admitted to hospital, basic functions such as walking and talking were beyond me.

I had not been able to walk straight and my speech was slurred.

But when Christ came into my life, he made me a 'new creation', changing me not only on the inside, but outside also. One of the first things that I did after my conversion was to pay a visit to the barber's. I emerged with my hair cropped army-style! My eyes were improving, the swelling in my face went down and I started to lose weight. As I got stronger my co-ordination began to return and I walked and talked properly. All in all, I developed a new attitude to my physical well-being. The Bible says that our bodies are the 'temples of the Holy Spirit'. As I realized this, I began to look after myself. With each new day I gained more and more strength, so finally I decided to return to work—at a taxi office on the Shankill Road.

The day I stepped outside my house to go back to work for the first time will be etched in my memory for ever. The weeks I had spent indoors praying and getting better had seen the season change from summer to autumn. It was a brisk morning. The golden leaves crunched underfoot as I made my way down the road. Young mothers pushed prams of smiling babies, old women with headscarves and shopping-bags nattered at street corners, middle-aged men dressed in overalls, lunch-boxes under arm, waited impatiently at the bus stop, hoping they would make it to work before the factory horn sounded, and throngs of children chattered excitedly as they hurried to school. During my weeks of torment and struggle life had gone on as normal. I was back in the midst of reality and I was sober.

Again Satan kept tormenting me, telling me I wouldn't be able to cope without a glass in my hand. But as I strolled down the Shankill I just kept repeating: 'I can do all things through Christ who strengthens me.'

As I got nearer to the office where I worked, I had to pass an old drinking haunt of mine, the Rex Bar. Because of the redevelopment on the Shankill, the Rex was one of only a few bars left open. Immediately it seemed to stand out from its surroundings. It was only a small bar, no bigger than a house, but it took on the proportions of the Empire State Building. An intensely powerful magnetic force tried to pull me into the bar and back into the web of booze and destruction. Voices shot through my head, 'You can have a drink. One won't hurt,' they shouted. 'You know you want one. Go on, yield to temptation!' I was shaking and sweating and felt very weak. Suddenly I realized that I was under attack from the enemy. I began to quote to myself, 'I can do all things through Christ who strengthens me.' The attack continued for about five minutes, but I stood my ground, repeating this verse. At last I was victorious and was able to proceed to my office.

At that time I gained much of my strength and confidence from spending time in God's house, the church of my boyhood, the Shankill Church of God. Sally was a member there and for many years that congregation had earnestly prayed for me to come back to God. It was strange going back for the first time. So many years had passed since I had walked through those doors, so much had happened. My life had been destroyed and rebuilt. As I climbed up the winding staircase leading into the main sanctuary I met Margaret Quail, a lady whom I had known as a boy. She looked at me in disbelief and ran away, frightened. Later she told me that she had found my appearance 'too much of a miracle'. She was simply astounded that a man like me could change so radically. But nothing is impossible with God, and many members of that church were encouraged by the power of God in my life.

It was marvellous to be worshipping amongst old familiar faces and to meet some new ones. In a sense, it was as if I had never been away. I had always been nervous about praying in public. Now that I had been stripped of the booze, a lot of my confidence had shrivelled up. But suddenly, one night in the prayer meeting I felt a strong compulsion to thank God for his work in my life. I rose slowly to my feet, my knees knocking, and feebly said,

'Lord, thank you for saving me. Thank you for bringing me into the kingdom of God.'

A short prayer, but a heartfelt one. At another prayer meeting I was so enthusiastic and excited that I jumped to my feet and, not realizing what I was saying, shouted, 'God bless you, Jesus!'

I could find no other way to express my praise to Jesus. The prayer meetings were a great source of power and strength to me and every Monday I was eager for eight o'clock to come so that I could get into God's house. As I prayed I really felt that I was doing business with God and that my life and the lives of others were changing. I was there as a result of prayer, but I needed continual prayer that God would sustain me in my new life with him.

Christmas was approaching and there were to be special services in the church. The pastor asked me if I would be prepared to talk about what had happened to me at one of the meetings and I said yes. Although I was extremely nervous about sharing my faith in public, I felt that I owed God a lot. This was the least I could do for him.

I remember standing on the platform looking down on the sea of faces. I cleared my throat and began talking, my voice trembling slightly. I told the people where God had brought me from, the kind of life that I had led. Then I simply praised and thanked God for his goodness. It was a nerve-racking experience and very emotional. I finished by reading part of Psalm 116:

'I love the Lord, for he heard my voice;
He heard my cry for mercy.
Because he turned his ear to me,
I will call upon him as long as I live.'

All this was a sharp contrast with my previous appearance in the Church of God just a few years before. I had staggered in, straight from the pub, and sat in the back row. All around I could hear whispers, 'Billy McIlwaine's in!'

I saw Sally sitting a few rows in front of me and suddenly she got up out of her seat and came to sit beside me. She was obviously embarrassed at my drunken state, but I suppose her love for me and her desire to see me come to Christ enabled her to overcome the humiliation. Going into God's house drunk was nothing to be proud of, but I believe that even in the depths of alcoholism God was speaking to me.

When alcohol had been the master of my life, it had destroyed many things, but now they were being restored. One of these was my relationship with my wife and daughter. For years Sally and I had lived in the same house, but we had lived as strangers. We had separate lives: mine built around pubs; hers around church. Now we had to learn to live together again, we had to get to know each other. It wasn't all smooth sailing; there were many tensions and conflicts. But with time and patience we ironed them out.

In 1981 we were able to afford our first holiday together. We decided to go to Spain. This was a brand new venture and it was great to enjoy each other's company without the booze. Because my money was no longer being squandered on alcohol, our standard of living went up. We moved into a bigger house and bought a second-hand caravan by the sea. But one of the greatest joys we were able to share together was going to church. No longer did Sally feel awkward about her family, now she had her husband with her and we were united in Christ.

I began to get to know my daughter as well. I had missed much of Rhonda's childhood and I couldn't change that. But now I wanted to be a father and a friend to her. For most of her life she had never seen me sober; we had never talked. I knew nothing of her life, her school, her friends. But now I wanted to share in what she had learned in history class, who her best friend was, the joy of a new pair of shoes. I thanked God that I was now able to share in the day-to-day trials and joys of family life.

After kicking the booze I had to go back to the hospital for periodic check-ups, during which they did some tests and X-rays. About a year after my conversion I found myself in the hospital for yet another check-up. After several hours of monotonous testing, my doctor turned to me, a look of total amazement on his face.

'Mr McIlwaine, something quite remarkable has happened,' he began. 'We have done extensive testing on your liver and it is totally whole! I can find absolutely nothing wrong with you.'

Earlier that morning I'd been telling the doctor about my supernatural conversion experience. He remembered this.

'We can't explain your healing,' he said, 'but you know in your own heart what you told me.'

That doctor wouldn't state that I had been supernaturally healed, but I knew in my own heart that God had touched my diseased liver and made it whole. I was overjoyed at God's goodness and mercy in my life. It was almost exactly a year ago that he had graciously allowed me to live and promised me complete healing. He had been true to his word. This step forward strengthened my relationship with God. I was determined never to go back to my old way of life, I was his child for ever.

The fact that God had really made me into a new creation was really brought home to me one day in the High Court. I bumped into Dennis Stewart, a QC I had known before I was a Christian. Mr Stewart happened to see me standing in a room with my friend John Chambers. He asked John who I was.

'You know very well that's Billy McIlwaine,' replied John.

But Mr Stewart refused to believe him. He asked me to stand nearer the window but still couldn't believe that I was Billy McIlwaine.

'You look completely different,' he told me. 'Your features are completely changed, your eyes are different, your voice is different.'

He was not only totally astounded by my appearance but also by the change in my attitude. Dennis Stewart at that time did not believe in God in the same way as myself, but was interested in Eastern religion. Yet he made a very remarkable statement.

'You look like a man who's been born again,' he said.

This man had seen me at the lowest ebb of my life. Many times I had passed him in court-rooms with a bottle of whisky in my pocket. Every single time we had met I had been under the influence of drink or, as he called it, 'firewater'.

So as he looked at me in this sunlit room he couldn't believe the transformation which had taken place. Indeed, we met many times after that and again and again he told me: 'I only have to look at you to know that you're still going on with the same way of life.'

I had been through a war—every attack, every battle had been fought with the sword of God's word and the armour of faith. God had been with me every step of the way, leading me into glorious victory—where even a man who failed to acknowledge God could see his glory reflected in me and comment: 'You're like a man who's been born again.'

16

Reaching Out

About a year after my conversion, I came to a decision: I needed to extend the same hand of love and mercy to others that God had stretched out to me. It was time for me to begin to live out that vow made in a hospital bed the previous summer. I had to be 'about my Father's business'.

Alcoholics Anonymous seemed to be a good starting-point. Feeling that I had something very positive to offer those struggling with alcoholism, I began to attend a local AA to share my story. Some members were trying to give up the booze in their own strength. I knew this was totally impossible; I tried and I'd failed.

The first night that I attended AA I sat and listened to story after story. The meeting was informal: we sat in a circle; some people just uttered a few words; others poured out their souls. I sat silent. The leader of the group then turned to me.

'Would you like to say anything, Billy?'

'Yes, I would,' I said.

This was the first of many nights on which I would share my own dramatic story. I tried to bring home the point that men and women could only live a fulfilling life, free of alcohol, through the power of God. My comments were met with sceptical remarks. Some people at the meeting resented me and didn't like me talking about Jesus Christ. They saw my words as an intrusion into their way of life. However, others gave me nothing but encouragement.

'You've got the right story; you've got something to offer people like us,' they said. 'Please keep coming back.'

Sometimes after the meetings people would come to me for counselling. I'm not saying they always wanted to accept Christ, but they always wanted to hear more. People were desperate, clutching at straws, anything to keep them off the booze.

One thing I have realized about alcoholism is that it is no respecter of persons. It goes beyond the boundaries of age, sex, and social class. It doesn't matter if you are a high-flying businessman or a building site labourer, male or female, teenager or senior citizen; you can become an alcoholic.

As well as going to AA meetings, I visited the local psychiatric hospital, Purdysburn. Robert Moore was one of the patients with whom I came in contact. He was a professor at Queens University and he was an alcoholic. Like many others he could not understand why this horrible disease was attacking him.

'Look, Billy,' he said to me, 'I can understand why perhaps uneducated people like yourself turn to alcoholism. But I have everything—intelligence, a great job and money. So why am I an alcoholic?'

'I really can't answer that, Dr Moore,' I replied. 'But what I do know is that alcohol is no respecter of persons, no one is immune from its clutches.'

I began to share with him how God had changed my life and delivered me from the booze. Although he listened intently, nothing dramatic like conversion happened. On my next visit I brought him the book *The Power of Positive Thinking*—still no signs of change, still he would not surrender his life to Christ.

But this time he began to share a little more about his drink problem.

'I managed to stay off the drink for a while,' he told me. 'But recently I went over to England to see my son. He's studying at university and had won a major chess championship, so we went out for a celebration meal and I thought I'd have a glass of table wine. I really didn't think it would do me any harm, but it's because of that one little drink that I'm here.'

The professor's story is one of many. One drink led to another and another and once again the desire for alcohol became uncontrollable. Once this professor had got a taste of alcohol he could not stop himself. I chatted with Dr Moore a few more times, but the last I heard of him was that after leaving the hospital his flat had burned down and he had escaped by the skin of his teeth.

Jim Stevens, Sally's brother, was another whose life was gripped by alcohol. I took him to AA and gospel meetings and tried to encourage him in every way I knew. Jim had been a good man, he had a lovely wife and a wonderful family. He was always respectable and well dressed. In his younger days he had worked as a foreman in one of the local timber yards and his wife had worked in the office. Jim and Betty seemed to be the perfect couple until alcohol took over their lives.

At first they were social drinkers and spent a few hours in the local pubs at weekends. But then they started to indulge a little bit more and then more, until alcohol became their way of life. In 1982 Betty died. She had been a beautiful woman, but alcohol had bloated her face and body. Jim was left alone in an empty flat, heavy with the memories of his dead wife. The bottle seemed to offer comfort. I tried to help him and at times he managed to kick the booze. But it never lasted long and Jim soon returned to his old haunts. I couldn't understand why what had worked for me didn't seem to be working for him. I'd had many successes with alcoholics, but I was puzzled about Jim.

The last time I saw Jim was in Belfast's Whiteabbey Hospital in December 1987. He lay, a mere shadow of a man, his body yellow and emaciated, at death's door. I thank God that Sally and I were given an opportunity to speak to him one last time. Later a neighbour told us he had turned to Christ. A short time later he died. The doctor admitted that alcohol had killed him.

David King was in his late fifties and an extremely successful businessman. He dealt in Waterford crystal and expensive china. He had a nice car and a beautiful home, but he was an alcoholic. Soon the business was on a downward slope. Inefficiency came creeping in as David became more interested in how many whiskies he could drink, rather than keeping his books in order. Profits usually ended up in the till of a bar or off-licence. One afternoon I received a call from his cousin, a solicitor, asking me if I could help this man. I agreed.

Our first meeting was turbulent. I confronted him immediately with his condition.

'You're an alcoholic!' I told him.

Right away his defences sprang up and resentment set in.

'Just who do you think you are to talk to a man like me in that way?' he shouted.

'Look, David, I don't think I'm anybody. I'm simply stating a fact,' I replied. 'Hold out your hands. Now look at the sweat—and you're shaking. You need a drink!'

'I'm not an alcoholic. I don't drink spirits, I stick to Guinness.'

'The only reason you drink Guinness,' I said, 'is that you've no money. If you had the cash, you'd be drinking the hard stuff, the shorts—the whisky and the vodka.'

Again I could see the anger rise in him.

'Look, David, I'm here to help you. If you don't want help that's up to you.'

I left. A few days later the phone rang. It was David. 'I need your help, Billy,' he said.

I felt that David should go into hospital for treatment, so I told him to get a note from his doctor to take to Purdysburn, the psychiatric hospital, where he could get dried out. Again the resentment and pride crept in. I suppose he felt that Purdysburn was too common, because he wanted to go to another hospital with a better reputation. But I told him that he wouldn't get accepted there and I was right.

So David was admitted to Purdysburn for the drying-out process. He managed to get through it and the hospital wanted to release him, but he had no home to go to. His wife had left him, no one wanted to know him, he was alone in the world. Because he had no place to go, he ended up in a ward for mentally disturbed people. Day and night he was forced to endure the rantings and ravings of the patients. Finally he got a flat and was able to leave Purdysburn.

David was able to stay off booze for long periods, so he went back into employment. But he never accepted Christ and I could do nothing about that. In the end the lure of the booze became too powerful for him to resist, and he lost his job as he was sucked back into the grip of alcohol.

I really feel that, if people would only realize the devastating effects which alcohol has on people's lives, then there would be fewer alcoholics. Alcoholism brings death and injury, the breaking of marriages, and poverty. And alcohol kills a lot more people than major drugs such as heroin, LSD or cocaine. The irony is that, unlike these substances, alcohol is socially acceptable. While drugs are illegal and the government puts health warnings on cigarette packets, people continue to drink freely without any restrictions. Alcohol is poisonous—emotionally, physically and mentally. It attacks the nervous system, liver and many other areas of the body.

I had to come to terms with failure to change people's lives for the better. In the end it is up to them to accept or reject what is on offer. Eric Black was someone I tried to help. I'd known him for a long time and he had seen me change from chronic alcoholic to someone totally delivered from alcohol's grip through the power of Jesus Christ. Eric's life was also steeped in booze and he wanted to get away from it. We had many conversations and I tried to encourage him. I took him to gospel meetings, bought him a Bible and took him home with me for meals. Eric was 'dry' and doing well. But as soon as the first problem came along he went back to his old lifestyle. This happened more than once. I would bump into him on the Shankill Road and he would be drunk. This sort of thing discouraged me and I found myself thinking, 'Lord, what am I doing wrong?' I'd really been praying, and asking God for his help and guidance for Eric. And I came to the conclusion that I wasn't going to be successful with every person that I encountered. Although it was a hard truth to grasp, I knew that when this happened I had to let go. There were other people that I needed to help. So I let Eric go and to this day, if he's still alive, he's probably still getting drunk.

One afternoon I was walking down the Shankill Road when I saw a familiar figure staggering towards me. He was quite old, scruffily dressed and stoned out of his mind. I hadn't seen Eddie since my drinking days and it seemed that very little had changed for him. I stopped to say hello and began to talk to him about Jesus. But I hadn't been talking for very long when he let out a laugh and began to mock and curse me. I was hurt at his reaction. I was a new Christian and eager to share my faith with him, but he did not want to listen. I began to feel sorry for Eddie. What I didn't know was it was the last time he would make fun of anyone sharing the gospel. Later that day he went home very drunk and started to beat up his wife. After years of abuse the woman had probably come to the end of her tether. This time she fought back. She lifted a large kitchen knife and stuck it in her husband. Eddie died.

I sometimes wonder if there is demon possession attached to alcoholism. I can't prove it, but if you look at the compulsion which drives the life (and destruction) of an alcoholic, you can see that he or she has no control over their actions. The whole personality changes.

I remember arriving late at an AA meeting one night. Even before I walked into the meeting room I could hear someone ranting and raving. I took a seat and began to listen. He was a tall thin man, pale and gaunt. He stood shouting and waving his arms around, muttering about his girlfriend. Then suddenly he announced that he was going to shoot her.

'I'm sick of that cow!' he yelled. 'She hates me and I hate her! I'm gonna kill her, one of these days I'm gonna put her out of her misery!'

I was disgusted by this whole episode. People didn't want to hear that kind of thing. They wanted to hear something which would help them. Several days later I went to another meeting in a different part of Belfast. At the opening of the meeting we were asked to stand for a minute's silence as a mark of respect for a member who had killed himself and his girlfriend. The man had shot his girlfriend and then turned the gun on himself. I was stunned and horrified that a man could have been driven so far by the booze.

Many people might say that you couldn't put the killings down to alcohol, but, in my experience, you can put anything down to alcohol. It warps the mind to such an extent that people often don't know what reality is. They can't differentiate between fact and fiction. Not every alcoholic is insane, but certainly all alcoholics go through times of insanity.

One Sunday night I took an alcoholic friend of mine to a gospel meeting. He seemed to be listening intently during the service and I prayed that God would speak to him. As I drove him to his home in east Belfast after the service we began to talk.

'Tommy, did you enjoy it tonight?' I asked.

'Yeah,' was all that he said.

'Well,' I continued, trying to get him to elaborate, 'wouldn't you like to accept Christ?'

'I suppose I would, Billy, but I need a sign. I need God to speak to me directly,' Tommy replied.

At that point the conversation was cut short as we had arrived at his house.

He asked me in for a cup of tea. We got out of the car and Tommy went to ring the doorbell. His wife soon appeared. She was distraught. Her face was red and tear-stained and she was shaking. She wasn't able to tell us what had happened for a few minutes. But we sensed that something very strange had taken place; the house seemed to be in utter turmoil. When she had calmed down, Tommy's wife began to unfold the bizarre events of that evening.

'About ten past seven, Lee [their son] picked up a Bible and, just as he was about to read it, something—I don't know what—some kind of force attacked him and threw him over the top of the settee!'

We were astounded, Tommy particularly, because

he told me that about ten past seven that night he had been sitting in that gospel meeting contemplating whether or not he should accept Christ. While he was trying to decide, it seemed that Satan, the enemy, wanted to have one last fling and had attacked his little boy.

I wasn't sure what to do about it all, but I knew that I had to do something. I decided to call my pastor to seek his advice. He told me to read the Bible in the room where Lee had been attacked, and to pray for Jesus in his mercy to help us.

As I entered the room I was immediately gripped by a piercing coldness. It was like being trapped inside a fridge. Quickly I flicked open the Bible. I wasn't sure what to read, so I prayed that the Bible would fall open at a suitable place. Psalm twenty-three lay before me, so I began to speak those beautiful words penned by King David. Afterwards Tommy's wife told me that their son had been reading the same psalm when he was attacked. I prayed and asked for the protection of Jesus to cover the room and the family. As I did this the awful coldness began to subside and a sense of peace began to fill the room. Then I went to the little boy's room and again read the Bible and prayed. But this time as I prayed the whole family got down on their knees and accepted Christ. Tommy had received the sign he needed.

That was the last I heard of that family until about five years later. I was ill at the time, suffering from angina. During the early hours of the morning the phone rang and the man at the other end said he was a police constable.

'Hello, Mr McIlwaine? We're holding a man here who's anxious to talk to you. Would you be able to come down to the station?'

'I'm sorry, constable,' I replied weakly. 'I'm ill right now, so there's no way I can come.'

The policeman went on to tell me that just a few hours earlier this man had tried to throw himself off the Queen's Bridge and, if it hadn't been for a passing police patrol, he would have been dead. That man was Tommy McFadden, whom I had led to Christ five years earlier. I learnt later that Tommy had allowed the devil to take hold of his mind once again and he had once more become ensnared in alcoholism. In the end, he had felt that there was nothing worth living for.

This brought home to me the fact that, to be really delivered from the grip of alcoholism, an individual has to be prepared to engage in warfare. After all, the booze has been the master and controller of the alcoholic's life for a long time, and the old master will not give up without a fight. It is a daily struggle, and no one is delivered from the grip of alcoholism overnight. It may be tempting to give up at the first problem, but you must be determined to go on with God, to read the Bible, to pray constantly and spend time with other Christians. Liberation does not come on a half-hearted basis. For many it's a long-drawn-out process and it can take years to get the victory. And don't deceive yourself—just that one little drink can do no end of harm. There's an old saying: 'One drink is one too many and a thousand is not enough.'

If you admit that you're an alcoholic and ask God for strength to resist that terrible compulsion, he can give it to you. You can't do it alone, but he is able.

17

On His Majesty's Service

It was now 1982—three years had passed since my conversion. I was still spending time helping alcoholics.

Several people including myself got together, called ourselves the United Evangelical Churches and planned to hold a gospel crusade. In August 1982 our ideas became a reality. For five nights the crowds thronged into the Stadium Recreation Centre on the Shankill Road, the place we had chosen as our venue. There was a spate of conversions and healings. Several people who were struggling with alcohol came up to me after the meeting. One man who had been 'dry' for several years told me that he felt that something was missing in his life. He needed *something* to fill that void which abstinence from the booze had created and that night he found the answer to his emptiness—Jesus. Other people to whom I talked committed their lives to Christ. It was an amazing time, as we saw God move in a mighty way.

But although the crusade was a success, there was one negative aspect. The meetings had been held in a predominantly Protestant area. This meant that it was extremely difficult and dangerous for people from Republican areas such as the Falls Road to attend.

As those of us who had organized the crusade prayed together, we decided to hold our next one in the Ulster

Hall in the centre of Belfast. This meant that people from all areas of the city could come. This opportunity to reach a greater cross-section of the community brought an added dimension.

The Ulster Hall crusade went on as planned and was a great success. From the opening night God's Spirit was at work showing people the truth about themselves, challenging and changing them. Over the next three evenings many more people, from both Catholic and Protestant backgrounds, realized that their respective 'religions' could not save them, only Jesus could. The meetings were also marked by miraculous healings.

1984 heralded a new development in my life. After an article about me appeared in *Buzz* Magazine (now *21st Century Christian*), I was approached by Lion Publishing Company with the offer of doing a book. After a lot of prayer I decided to go ahead with this and by the end of the year *An End to Terrorism* appeared in bookshops all over Britain. The launching of the book was greeted with a great deal of press and television coverage. Many people found Christ for themselves through that book, which gave me tremendous joy.

There had been one point in my early Christian life when I was tempted to return to alcohol. One Friday night towards the end of 1981 I was getting ready for bed when suddenly I heard a loud explosion. Although it seemed pretty close, I didn't flinch, it was just another bomb blast, just another tragedy in Ulster's mindless spate of deaths and injuries. But I was wrong. This time the troubles had touched my own family.

Half an hour later the phone rang. It was my sister May to tell me the awful news that her son-in-law, a policeman, had been blown up at Unity Flats. William Coulter was only twenty-three when he died, leaving my young pregnant niece a widow. His death sparked off one of the biggest trials I've ever had to face in my Christian life.

I experienced a strong pull back towards the booze. My immediate reaction was to blot out the terrible reality of it all. For twenty years, when difficult situations arose, I had resorted to alcohol, so now it was hard to turn away. I found myself consumed once more with bitterness. When I talked to other Christians, I asked them to pray for me. Those prayers were powerful, because God removed those old desires from my heart once more. He gave me a spirit of forgiveness and I was actually able to pray for the conversion of those men who had killed William.

I often have to explain to people that the Christian life is not plain sailing. Difficult situations are going to arise that will tempt us to return to the old way of life. But if we cling to God he will help us to resist the enemy.

In 1983 another tragedy occurred. A few years previously I would have responded to it by returning to the alcohol. This was when Mountain Lodge, a tiny church in the heart of Armagh bandit country, was viciously sprayed with bullets during a Sunday evening service. Three church elders were shot dead and many others were injured. Having preached in this church, I knew a few of the people there very well, so this news sent shock waves through me. Immediately I got on the phone to Jimmy Burney, a close friend of mine, who had been at that fateful service. He cried as he told me the events of that night. I felt I should go down there to offer any help or support that I could. This time, instead of wanting to bury my head in the booze, I longed to be an instrument of God's love.

I drove to Jimmy's house. People there from Mountain Lodge were numb with the shock of the night's events. I tried to offer sympathy and prayers. It was hard to know what to say in such a situation.

The next night we drove in to Mountain Lodge. The tiny church was in utter chaos and there was a strong sense of evil in the air. The floor was streaked with blood and a series of bullet holes cut deep into the concrete walls. They were dark and terrible days, but God got the glory. There was no bitterness from those who had suffered bereavement. They expressed nothing but worship for Jesus, knowing that their loved ones were with him.

In 1985 something happened which threatened to destroy my life and my relationship with God. In the early months of that year, I was driving back from Dublin when suddenly I was stricken with severe chest pains. Sharp spasms of pain shot up my arms and down my spine. I writhed in torment and found it almost impossible to drive. By the next day I was once again confined to a hospital bed, and after intensive testing was told that I was suffering from angina. For much of 1985 Satan once more wove his web of lies and deception. 'You're finished,' he told me. 'You're going to die! You will never speak to anyone else about Jesus and you won't travel ever again.'

These words ate away at me, turning me into an emotional and physical cripple, unable to do anything that required any great effort. Recurring chest pains put me back in hospital a few more times that year and it seemed that my life was ebbing away in front of my eyes. The pill bottle became my new master. I was ruled by a constant stream of tablets that I was forced to pump into my system daily—one lot to slow down my heartbeat and another lot to open my arteries.

1986 swung around and God began to pull me out of that dark pit into which I had been sinking. An American evangelist called Richard Roberts came to

Belfast and I decided to go along with a friend to hear what he had to say. I have to confess that I went with a sceptic's heart. When Roberts spoke about healing, that he was a powerful and challenging speaker. Yet I looked at my own situation and thought, 'Well, God's not healing me.' I was still a Christian, but I felt that God had deserted me. My prayers were unanswered, and now they seemed just empty words, lacking in power and producing no results. Despite my cynicism I decided to fill in a card during the meeting, in order to receive a book from Richard Roberts.

Some days later I came downstairs to find a small brown package lying in the hallway. That particular morning I was at an extremely low ebb, the drugs I was on were not helping and my condition was deteriorating once again. But just as I was sinking to my lowest, God was lifting me up. That package contained a book called *The God of a Second Chance* by Richard Roberts. As I tore open the brown paper I felt the Holy Spirit say to me, 'Make this your point of contact, like the woman who touched Jesus' garment. Receive your healing.'

Immediately I placed my hands on the book and started to pray. I told God, 'I'm going to believe you for my healing, instead of these drugs. I'm coming off them!'

I want to emphasize that I don't advocate that people stop taking drugs just like that. It can be very foolish and dangerous. But I was compelled to take that step of faith.

I sent for the doctor and told him my decision. The drugs had been having bad side-effects, causing headaches and pressure at the back of my neck.

'Look, Mr McIlwaine, I would strongly advise against withdrawal,' the doctor told me. 'These pills are necessary to stabilize your condition. If you stop taking them, who knows what will happen?'

But I was determined to stick to my decision. I felt that my life was totally resting in God's hands as I spoke out the verse from the Old Testament: 'By his wounds we are healed.' Jesus had died on the cross not only for our sins but also for our sicknesses and I clung to this promise.

Although I felt I had been healed, my body still manifested the symptoms of disease. But when people inquired how I was feeling, I started to reply that I was healed. Even when excruciating pains shot up and down my chest and arms, I refused to acknowledge them to others. Instead I confessed my healing through the power of Jesus Christ.

Six weeks later I went to the Royal Victoria Hospital for a check-up. Before beginning tests the doctor asked me how I was feeling. I told him what I had told everyone else.

'I believe I'm healed.'

He looked at me, puzzled. 'What makes you think that?' he asked abruptly.

Again I said, 'I really believe that God has healed my body of angina.'

He stared at me sceptically, as doctors do when you begin to talk in this way.

'Well, we'll soon find out,' he said.

I was put through a rigorous set of tests: a deep heart scan, blood tests and the treadmill.

Two weeks later the results of my tests came through and I returned to the hospital. What I had known all along was confirmed that day. The same doctor told me that I wouldn't need any more drugs or hospital visits; my angina had completely disappeared.

God had restored me to full health. Once again I could be on His Majesty's Service.

18

New Pastures

When one door closes another opens. In a sense this saying sums up my Christian life.

During the course of my illness I had started to lose direction. I had been involved in working with alcoholics for so long, this was my thing, this was what God had called me to. It was hard to know what I should do. Where would I go from here? I took my concerns to God.

'Lord, do you want me to continue or do you want me to do something different?' I asked.

There was no immediate answer, no flashes of lightning came from heaven. I realized that I had to wait for God to answer.

One day as I was flicking through a magazine, an advertisement squeezed into the top corner of a page suddenly caught my eye. It was promoting a three-month Bible course in England. The aim was to enhance Bible knowledge and to prepare people to become church ministers. I'd never really considered a full-time Bible course before, but this ad really seemed to leap out at me. I felt compelled to apply and I knew the outcome would somehow determine which direction my life would take.

Initially I was refused admission to the course, because of a lack of accommodation. But this problem was soon ironed out. Sally's cousin and her husband lived in England so I decided to move in with them while I took the course.

I managed to get leave from work and so, in October 1986, I took the Larne/Stranraer Ferry and drove down into England to begin my three-month's study at Bethesda Pentecostal Church in Bury. It was tough wrenching myself from my family, but I knew that I was doing God's will.

The course was intensive and required determination and commitment. But I gained a great deal from the teachers and also from the other men in the class. I felt that I would really be able to put these new skills to use when I returned to Belfast. At that time I never considered that perhaps God was leading me into new work. About half-way through the course, one of the teachers challenged me on this point.

'Why don't you listen to the Spirit of God, to see where he wants you to go now?' he said.

Although I knew that this was the only way forward, I found it almost impossible to imagine living anywhere but Northern Ireland. My roots were so deep there. But I began to pray and fast and I tried to be open to God. One Saturday afternoon two fellow students and I drove over to Liverpool to buy some books. The city lay sprawling on the banks of the grey Mersey.

Later we walked through the streets of Toxteth. Among the derelict buildings and graffiti I saw a resilient people. They were people for whom every day was a struggle to survive, people who were crying out for God. I saw young kids haggling with drug pushers over the price of crack, old haggard men sprawled along the footpath with a bottle at their side. I realized that these people needed the same release from their bondage that I had experienced eight years before. Despite the chaos and sadness of this inner-city area, I felt the peace of God descend on me and I realized that he was clearly speaking to me about this troubled city.

I asked my friends if they had experienced any kind of peace about Liverpool.

'You must be joking! How could you possibly feel any peace here?' they said laughing.

As we walked back to the car park, I knew that I had had a personal revelation. I asked God if he would give me a sign.

'If you want me to come to Liverpool to work for you when the course is finished, put it in the hearts of the leaders to ask me to do some evangelism here.'

A few weeks later it was time for all of us to try to find the way forward for our lives. I shouldn't have been surprised—but when I was approached by some men from the Home Missions Council of the Assemblies of God who asked me if I would go to Liverpool to do some evangelistic work, I was astonished. I knew that, although it would be painful, I would have to uproot myself and leave my beloved Northern Ireland. For the time being my work there was finished, God wanted me in Liverpool.

But I was not the only person involved in this upheaval. I knew that God would have to work in the hearts of my wife and daughter. When I first discussed this with my family neither Sally nor Rhonda wanted to leave Northern Ireland. But human reasoning crumbles when the Spirit of God moves in. All their negative attitudes were abandoned when God spoke to them. For Rhonda it had seemed impossible to accompany us to England. She had already applied to universities around Northern Ireland, and her principal had told her that to change to an English college would be extremely difficult at that late stage. But God swept aside that obstacle, and she was accepted at Manchester University.

So on 11 August 1987, a perfect day for sailing, we left the shores of Ireland for our new home across the Irish Sea. We quickly settled in Radcliffe, a small town outside Manchester. I started my new job in Liverpool and, over the eighteen months I was there, met leaders from many other churches. All of us, whatever our denomination, had one goal—to see people won for Christ.

Towards the end of my time in Liverpool we held a crusade in an area called Huyton. About sixty people came to Christ.

In May 1988, on a warm lazy Sunday afternoon, I was out in the garden basking in the sun. The phone rang and I dashed indoors to answer it. It was the Secretary of the Home Missions Council. 'Billy, how would you feel about working down in the Midlands for a while?'

I was surprised at this, because I had imagined working in Liverpool for a while longer. But I told him that I would pray about it. The Council was keen for me to build up a church in Warwick, a picturesque little town in the heart of Shakespeare country. At that time the church was floundering. It had practically wound down and only one or two faithful ladies continued to come to the Bible study held every Sunday. I knew that to pastor and build up a church would be a mammoth task. I also wondered about taking on the role of a pastor. I had always felt that I was an evangelist, but I suppose that God had different ideas. After much prayer, I had a very definite word from him, 'Go!'

I obeyed and began to pour my soul into building up a strong church for the glory of God. At the same time I found myself invited to preach in other churches around England, so in a sense God let me continue with my evangelistic ministry.

On my travels around different parts of England, one thing which has struck me is the way alcohol grips people's lives. It has imprisoned many people. Go into any town or city at the weekend and you will see throngs of young people staggering aimlessly around the streets, worse the wear for drink. Among older people alcohol abuse tends to be more covert. As in Northern Ireland, there are many, many people in England whose lives have been totally shattered by alcohol.

After eighteen months in Liverpool, I was now pastor of a church. The local psychiatric hospital had many alcoholics among its patients and I found myself spending long hours not only sharing my story, but also simply listening. Many of those patients were filled with pent-up frustration, needing the release that comes through talking to someone. In the church we have seen many of these people come through our doors and make the decision to follow Christ. To see individuals released from mental and physical bondage has been fantastic. Many of the people I visited were in one particular ward. It wasn't long before its doors were closed. I think that we, or rather God, put it out of business.

Billy McIlwaine, pastor, is a far cry from the long-haired, beer-bellied, pathetic character who used to stagger up the Shankill Road clutching his six-pack or bottle of whisky. I would never want anyone to experience those wasted hellish years that I spent steeped in alcohol. Yet millions of people around the world are experiencing the horrors of booze.

I've been sober over ten years now and it's been a decade of great inner peace. It has been great to live life without the aid of a bottle by my side. Many people have asked me if alcohol still poses a temptation. In answer to that I would say that drink no longer holds an attraction for me. I don't think that I will ever go back to that nightmarish life, but I still live one day at a time and depend on God for his help and strength. I've found him to be the alcoholic's answer, and now my thirst is for him and not for what I can get out of a whisky bottle.

Alcohol is a destroyer, it wrecks homes, families and businesses. Everything that it touches decays. Alcohol is a bigger killer, through cirrhosis of the liver, road accidents and suicides, than any of the other major drugs. A recent report by the Royal College of Physicians estimates the total number of deaths through alcohol-related conditions as ranging between 5,000 and 10,000 a year. And a recent estimate of the life-years lost through alcohol in England and Wales gives a low figure of 119,000 and a high figure of 192,000.

I would like to see a change of attitude towards alcohol by both the Government and society at large. Many people have the misleading idea that only a minority of the population is genetically and physically capable of becoming dependent on alcohol. Although genetic factors may be important, it is still impossible to identify which individuals are prone to alcohol dependence and those who are immune. Another misunderstanding which needs to be cleared up is that alcohol-related disease is confined to a relatively small number of individuals with 'skid row' problems of social and physical disintegration. Every human being is vulnerable to the lure of alcohol, or indeed to any other major drug. Each of us is born with a 'spiritual vacuum' inside us, a void which needs to be filled so that we can achieve some degree of satisfaction in life. Some people turn to possessions to bridge the gap, others to relationships, many turn to alcohol.

But Christians no longer have that terrible

emptiness, because Christ fills our lives, and he alone can satisfy. My prayer is that Christians will take a firm stand on righteousness and holiness and say no to alcohol. Yet it is important not to become proud or self-righteous in our attitude. After all, once upon a time that dirty unshaven man lying sprawled across the footpath was me. One day it could be you or a member of your family. Love the alcoholic, reach out to the alcoholic, but most important of all pray for the alcoholic, is my message. Only the power of God can purge the individual from the poison that warps his mind and body.

My belief is that the only way to make sure that you never become an alcoholic is never to take the first drink. There's always the possibility that, even if you only usually drink a little, when tragedy strikes or problems arise, you'll turn to the booze for comfort. I wasn't always an alcoholic, but the turbulent events of my life caused me to cross that dividing line between social drinker and alcoholic.

But even if you have crossed that dividing line, despite what you might think, you are not unreachable. In your own strength you will never truly escape the clutches of alcohol, but there is someone who can help you. Over ten years ago I adopted a motto to live by: 'I can do all things through Christ who strengthens me.'

More titles from Lion Publishing

HELL'S ANGEL
Brian Greenaway

Brian Greenaway was president of a Hell's Angel chapter. He was violent, full of hate, deeply into drugs.
 Then, in Dartmoor Prison, he had an experience which changed him completely.

This is Brian's own story—powerful, sometimes ugly but real. It describes his tough early years, his dramatic conversion and his struggles to work out a new way of life.

ISBN 0 85648 389 3

KILLING TIME
Noel Fellowes

Imagine your worst nightmare.

Arrested and interrogated for a murder you know nothing about.

Sentenced to years behind bars for a crime you did not commit.

But there's a final, chilling detail to this nightmare. You are an ex-policeman, hated by everyone in the 600-strong prison.

'It would be an understatement to say that this is an extremely disturbing case.'
The Lord Chief Justice, Lord Lane

'It is clear that police officers handling the case either ignored or deliberately withheld vital evidence.'
Sunday Express

ISBN 0 7459 1051 3

A selection of top titles from LION PUBLISHING

HELL'S ANGEL Brian Greenaway	£2.99 ☐
INSIDE Brian Greenaway	£2.99 ☐
KILLING TIME Noel Fellowes	£3.50 ☐
ON THE SIDE OF THE ANGELS John Smith	£2.99 ☐
COPING WITH DEPRESSION Myra Chave-Jones	£1.95 ☐
LISTENING TO YOUR FEELINGS Myra Chave-Jones	£3.99 ☐
LOVE NEVER ENDS Jenny Richards	£2.99 ☐
FOR THE LOVE OF SANG Rachel Anderson	£3.99 ☐
IRINA Dick Rodgers	£2.50 ☐
SHADOW OF WAR Gerda Erika Baker	£3.99 ☐
FACE TO FACE WITH CANCER Marian Stroud	£3.95 ☐
THE LONG ROAD HOME Wendy Green	£1.95 ☐
WHOSE PROMISED LAND? Colin Chapman	£4.99 ☐

All Lion paperbacks are available from your local bookshop or newsagent, or can be ordered direct from the address below. Just tick the titles you want and fill in the form.

Name (Block letters)

_____

Address

_____

_____

_____

Write to Lion Publishing, Cash Sales Department, PO Box 11, Falmouth, Cornwall TR10 9EN, England.

Please enclose a cheque or postal order to the value of the cover price plus:

UK: 80p for the first book, 20p for each additional book ordered to a maximum charge of £2.00.

OVERSEAS INCLUDING EIRE: £1.50 for the first book, £1.00 for the second book and 30p for each additional book.

BFPO: 80p for the first book, 20p for each additional book.

Lion Publishing reserves the right to show on covers and charge new retail prices which may differ from those previously advertised in the text or elsewhere, and to increase postal rates in accordance with the Post Office.